Direct Contact by God

Inspired Homilies:
Rev. Roderick C. Davis

plus

Exciting Firsthand Experiences
Divine Dreams and Visions

of

Russell and Paul Maddock

by

Reverend Roderick C. Davis

Davis Associates Publishing
Las Vegas, Nevada

Annette Munnich, Publicist, Bourbonnais, ILL, designed the front cover, and Davis Associate Publishing prepared the interior for publication.
The Miracle of Three Physical Signs from God / Reverend Roderick C. Davis.
Publisher: Davis Associates Publishing; Second Edition (April 15, 2015)
Language: English.

PREFACE

Four resources were utilized in the preparation of the Homilies by Rev. Roderick C. Davis, and also in the Holy Spirit guided explanation of the Divine Dreams and Visions of Russell and Paul Maddock. The resources are: the Catholic Bible, Douay Version; the King James Bible, KJV; the Gospel of the Holy Twelve; and The Clementine Homilies.

Biblical references to certain information given in the Homilies, have not been included in this writing, but they are provided in 'The Miracle of Three Physical Signs from God,' written by Rev. Roderick C. Davis, and purchase details of the eBook, and hard and softcover editions, are in Chapter 20, 'Resources for Further Study, and Other Information.'

The Gospel of the Holy Twelve, Jesus' Gospel, fully referenced in 'The Miracle of Three Physical Signs from God, and translated from the Aramaic, is one of the most ancient and complete fragments of the Jewish Christian Movement. Based upon historical records, Apostle John recorded his Jesus' Gospel while incarcerated. Once completed, he made it known to the other Apostles, and then to protect it from falsification, a trusted disciple took the Gospel to hide it in a Buddhist Monastery in Tibet. Proof the Apostles would have taken such a precaution is in Chapter II of Apostle Peter's epistle to Jesus' brother, James, Bishop of Jerusalem, that is within The Clementine Homilies, fully referenced in 'The Miracle of Three Physical Signs from God.'

Historical records disclose Fr. Placidus, when visiting the Buddhist Tibetan Monastery during the 1870's, where the Gospel had been hidden, asked if he could bring the fragments to Church Authorities in Rome, and they agreed. Placidus, in the time it took him to travel back to Rome, translated some of the Gospel into Latin, which he read to a gathering of Cardinals. However, when the Cardinals became aware of the fact the Gospel contained doctrine that had not been approved by the

i

First Council of Nicaea, 325 AD, they chose not to make it known; the reason being: they feared public knowledge of the Doctrine it contained, would have an adverse effect on the Church, and decided the fragments should be secreted within Vatican archives.

Fortunately, numerous fragments, over a period of time, were passed on by Emmanuel Swedenborg, Anna Kingsford, Edward Maitland, and Fr. Placidus, and per a biography written by Samuel Hopgood Hart, Reverend G. J. R. Ouseley, structured the Gospel of the Holy Twelve from the translated fragments.

I mentioned The Clementine Homilies, which is an extremely important ancient writing of Clement of Rome, a Church Father who had been personally trained in Jesus' Doctrine by Apostle Peter. Peter also appointed Clement to be a Church Father, and in addition to an epistle from Apostle Peter to Jesus' brother, James, and an epistle from Clement to James, it also contains a record of the lessons Apostle Peter preached. Why is it an extremely important writing? The information within the epistles and in the messages of the lessons Apostle Peter preached, mirror the messages of the lessons recorded by Apostle John, in Jesus' Gospel.

By cross referencing the Catholic Bible, Douay Version, and the King James Bible, KJV, with the Gospel of the Holy Twelve and The Clementine Homilies, one can prove beyond a shadow of a doubt, even though this information is not disclosed in the New Testament, the fact that Jesus did preach often that he would end the bloody sacrifices of the law. The information contained in the aforementioned writings, also proves beyond a shadow of a doubt, that the blood covenant of Exodus 24, and the blood sacrifice rituals and laws of Exodus 29, are not of God, but of men.

One last point before moving on: I utilized the King James Bible, KJV, and the Catholic, Douay Version, as my reference

sources, for I have found they are less corrupt than some of
the newer versions

TABLE OF CONTENTS

Chapter 1   1
Homily: How Deuteronomy 31:20-30 lessons tie to other lessons within other Books of the Old Testament, and the very important message they convey.

Chapter 2   7
Homily: How Zechariah lessons tie to other lessons within other Books of the Old Testament, and the very important message they convey.

Chapter 3   12
Homily: A discussion of the messages conveyed in Leviticus 1, as they apply other books within the Old Testament, and to lessons Jesus taught in His Gospel, and lessons Apostle Peter preached in The Clementine Homilies.

Chapter 4   18
Homily: A discussion of the messages conveyed in Amos 5, as they apply other books within the Old Testament, and to lessons Jesus and Apostle Peter taught.

Chapter 5   23
Homily: A discussion of: Psalms 22 prophecies which Jesus fulfilled; and why certain crucial lessons Jesus preached are not in the New Testament.

Chapter 6   30
Homily: How prophecies which Jesus fulfilled, apply in our daily lives.

Chapter 7   35
Homily: A discussion of the Lords condemnation of the blood sacrifice in Isaiah 1, as it applies to Jesus' Gospel recorded by Apostle John.

Chapter 8   43
Homily: A discussion of Isaiah 53 prophesies Jesus fulfilled, and other Old Testament prophecies that tie with Isaiah 53, which negate the grace and salvation preached by Pharisee Saul/Paul.

Chapter 9   51
Homily: A discussion of 2 Samuel 24 lessons as they apply to Jesus' Doctrine recorded by Apostle John.

Chapter 10   57
Gospel Reading: Ezekiel 2 & 4 - Reading from Jesus' Gospel:
Lesson 68 & 76.

Chapter 11   71
Homily Discussion of Deuteronomy Lessons, Chapters 1-12, as
they apply to lessons in Jesus' Gospel recorded by Apostle John.

Chapter 12   77
Homily: A discussion of Leviticus 16 lessons as they relate to
those taught by Jesus, as recorded by Apostle John.

Chapter 13   82
Homily: a discussion of Ecclesiastes 3 lessons as they apply to
Jesus' lessons taught as, recorded by Apostle John.

Chapter 14   86
Homily: A discussion of Micah Verses as they related to lessons
Jesus taught, as they were written by Apostle John.

Chapter 15   90
Homily: Discussion of Jeremiah lessons as they apply to lessons
Jesus' taught, as recorded by Apostle John, and those preached
by Pharisee Saul/Paul, and adopted as authorized church doctrine
by the First Council of Nicaea 325 AD.

Chapter 16   100
The Anointing of Russell and Paul Maddock as God's Prophets
and Two Witnesses

Chapter 17   115
The Ones That Don't Belong

Chapter 18   148
Warning: Punishment and Desolation

Chapter 19   187
Barren

Chapter 20   197
Resources for Further Study, and Other Information

Chapter 1

Homily: How Deuteronomy 31:20-30 lessons tie to other lessons within other Books of the Old Testament, and the very important message they convey.

Brothers and Sisters in Christ, I have been told that my sermons are different from those normally given, and I agree, my sermons *are* different. Why have I chosen to do such? It is because of two physical signs that God sent to me: one came during July of 2010; and the 2nd came in July of 2012, which I have fully disclosed on RodCDavis.com. God confirmed to me in both physical signs that He wants His true Word, and His Son's true Doctrine, to be brought to light.

Why is it important God's true Word and His Son's true Doctrine be brought to light? Some lessons contained in the Old and New Testaments of the King James and Catholic Bibles, do not teach the "Truth, as a ladder with many steps, for the salvation and perfection of the soul," that God gave to mankind, through the Holy Spirit, prophets, and His Son. The lessons to obtain forgiveness and salvation, as taught in the King James and Catholic Bibles, are very different from those that had been handed down by God.

Some lessons in today's reading of Deuteronomy, Chapter 31, can be linked to lessons within other Books of the Old Testament, which help to piece together a trail of evidence that makes clear, the Law given to Moses by the Lord, has been changed by men, to suit their needs and traditions. For instance, in Verse 20 the Lord told Moses, "then will they turn unto other gods, and serve them, and provoke me, and break my covenant." As you will soon learn, the Israelites *did* break the Lord's covenant.

Next, we are told in Verse 24 of Deuteronomy, Chapter 31, Moses wrote the words of the law, and then in Verses 25 and 26, he commanded the priests to put the book of the

1

law he wrote inside the Ark of the Covenant. Moses, in Verse 27, told the priests that they had been rebellious against the Lord, and in Verse 29 he told them he knew that after his death, they would utterly corrupt themselves, and turn away from the way in which he had commanded them through the law the Lord had given to him.

Verse 32 of Jeremiah, Chapter 31, crystallizes the fact that Moses' statement had been right on target, for Verse 32 tells us: "Not according to the covenant that I made with their fathers in the day that I took them by the hand to bring them out of the land of Egypt; which my covenant they break."

In addition, the Book of Isaiah provides further proof the Israelites broke God's covenant given to Moses. In Isaiah, Chapter 1, Verse 4, the Lord told Isaiah, "Ah sinful nation, a people laden with iniquity, a seed of evildoers, children that are corrupters: they have forsaken the LORD," and in Verse 11 the Lord said, "To what purpose is the multitude of your sacrifices unto me? saith the LORD: I am full of the burnt offerings of rams, and the fat of fed beasts; and I delight not in the blood of bullocks, or of lambs, or of he goats," and in Verse 12 the Lord asked Isaiah, "When ye come to appear before me, who hath required this at your hand?"

Further to that, in today's reading of Jesus' Gospel, Jesus told His chosen Twelve in Verse 11, "that which hath been taught by them of old time is true—though corrupted by the foolish imaginations of men." "That which hath been taught by them of old time is true," was the Gospel of Jesus' time, and today, that Gospel is known as the Old Testament.

Jesus' statement in Verse 11, is backed up even further by this statement Jesus made to the Pharisees, priests and scribes, in Lection 51, Verse 17, "against Moses indeed I do not speak nor against the law, but against them who

2

corrupted his law, which he permitted for the hardness of your hearts." The examples I have provided, prove beyond doubt, the Israelites changed God's Law, to suit their own needs and traditions.

I mentioned a little while ago that in Jeremiah, Chapter 31, Verse 32, the Lord told the Israelites they broke His covenant, and Jeremiah, Chapter 7, Verse 22, identified the covenant the Israelites broke, when the Lord said, "For I spake not unto your fathers, nor commanded them in the day that I brought them out of the land of Egypt, concerning burnt offerings or sacrifices."

Verse 15 in Lection 51, of today's reading of Jesus' Gospel, revealed to us the commandment God had given to Moses, that the Israelites eliminated, and replaced with the blood covenant of Exodus, Chapter 24, Verse 8, and the blood sacrifice laws within Exodus, Chapter 29. Verse 15 told us, "As also bear witness when he saith, concerning blood offerings and sacrifices I the Lord God commanded none of these things in the day that ye came out of Egypt, [and this section of the Verse gives the commandment the Lord gave to Moses] *but only this I commanded you to do, righteousness, walk in the ancient paths, do justice, love mercy, and walk humbly with thy God*.

In addition to the Old Testament lessons of today, there are a couple lessons within Lection 64 of Jesus' Gospel, that I want to bring to your attention, and they are in Verses 8 and 9. In Verse 8 we were told God sent forth the beloved Son, the divine Love, and the beloved Daughter, the holy Wisdom, and Verse 9 tells us they "descend to earth to dwell with men and teach them the ways of God, to love the laws of the Eternal, and obey them, that in them they may find salvation."

Jesus did not mention, or even hint in any manner whatsoever, in any of the lessons He preached throughout His Gospel, that His sacrifice in fulfillment of scripture, would redeem mankind from their sin. Actually He made it very clear that a soul must learn the ways of God, and love them, and obey them that in them they may find salvation, or in other words, obey them that they may *EARN* their salvation. That lesson is very different from the gift of salvation that is taught within the New Testaments of the King James and Catholic Bibles.

Before concluding, I want to bring to your attention a statement I made earlier, which is, "Truth, as a ladder with many steps, for the salvation and perfection of the soul." Jesus made that statement to His chosen Twelve in Lection 90, Verse 10, "God giveth you all Truth, as a ladder with many steps, for the salvation and perfection of the soul, and the truth which seemeth to day, ye will abandon for the higher truth of the morrow. Press ye unto Perfection." And then in Verse 11 He said, "Whoso keepeth the holy Law which I have given, the same shall save their souls."

Jesus' statement, "the truth which seemeth to day, ye will abandon for the higher truth of the morrow," conveys this important message: that which you think is truth today, you will no longer believe, for you will have found a new truth. What new truth? They were the new truths Jesus preached in fulfillment of scripture, which were contradictory to certain revered Hebrew Laws. Those truths indeed became the higher truth, as His resurrection proved beyond debate, that He truly is the Son of God.

The holy Law Jesus gave, as He stated in Lection 90, Verse 11, He gave in fulfillment of the Jeremiah 31:31 prophecy, wherein the Lord stated, "I will make a new covenant with the house of Israel." Jesus' statement that He made in His Sermon on the Mount, which is contained in Lection 25, Verse 8, confirms He gave the holy Law.

Jesus said in Verse 8, "But behold One greater than Moses is here, and he will give you the higher law, even the perfect Law, and this Law shall ye obey." Unfortunately,

4

none of the Laws He gave in fulfillment of prophecy are found within the New Testament, for they are contradictory to blood sacrifice Hebrew Laws that are found in Exodus, Chapter 29, wherein we are told that redemption from sin can be obtained through the blood sacrifice.

Contrary to the remission of sin through the blood sacrifice as told in Verses within Exodus, Chapter 29, Jesus told His chosen Twelve in Lection 33, Verse 2, "No blood offering, of beast or bird, or man, can take away sin, for how can the conscience be purged from sin by the shedding of innocent blood? Nay, it will increase the condemnation." And He told them in Verse 3, "The priests indeed receive such offering as a reconciliation of the worshippers for the trespasses against the law of Moses, but for sins against the Law of God there can be no remission, save by repentance and amendment."

Brothers and Sisters, there are those who vehemently defend that the King James and Catholic Bibles are true as written, and they absolutely refuse to lay eyes upon anything which can prove otherwise. Jesus told His chosen Twelve, children of the wicked one would be responsible for sowing tares in the good wheat He had given them to sow in the world, and He said things would be taught in His Name that He did not teach.

Apostle Peter personally trained early Church Father, Clement of Rome, in Jesus' Doctrine, and appointed Clement to be a Church Father. Clement recorded in his homilies that Apostle Peter accused children of the wicked one, of changing his Master's Doctrine. Peter, in his epistle to Jesus' brother, Apostle James, fretted what would become of His Master's Doctrine, when he would no longer be here to protect it.

Brothers and Sisters, as I have done before, I again appeal to you to please, become a warrior for God and His Son, and share with all those who will listen, God's and His Son's Truths, that I share with you.

Chapter 2

Homily: How Zechariah lessons tie to other lessons within other Books of the Old Testament, and the very important message they convey.

Brothers and Sisters in Christ, there are some lessons in today's reading of Zechariah, and also in Lection 44, of Jesus' Gospel recorded by Apostle John, that I want to discuss. The first is in Zechariah, Chapter 5, Verses 1 though 4, wherein the angel told Zechariah, after he had seen a flying roll, that it had been a curse over the face of the earth upon all those who steal, including every one that swears. Then the angel told Zechariah that it would enter into the house of the thief, and also the house of him that swear falsely by my name.

Those Verses provide extremely important information that ties very well with 2 John, Chapter 1, Verse 9, which states, "Whosoever transgresseth, and abideth not in the doctrine of Christ, hath not God. He that abideth in the doctrine of Christ, he hath both the Father and the Son." Why does it tie well?

Think about this: Verse 4 of Zechariah, Chapter 5, states, I will bring it forth, saith the LORD of hosts, and it shall enter into the house of him that sweareth falsely by my name;" being we know through lessons contained in the Gospel of the Holy Twelve, that the New Testament does not contain many of the important lessons Jesus preached, how then, can those who follow only the lessons in the King James and Catholic Bibles, swear other than falsely?

Further to that, who benefits by those who swear falsely? The wicked one! Why? Jesus told his chosen Twelve that children of the wicked one would be responsible for sowing tares in the good wheat that He gave them to sow in the world, and Apostle Peter, within The Clementine Homilies, confirmed it happened, and accused the children of the wicked one of being responsible.

Verses 12 and 13 and 15 of Zechariah, Chapter 6, tell us that a man whose name is The Branch, shall build the temple of the Lord, and he shall bear the glory, and be a priest and rule upon his throne, and that they who are far off shall come and build the temple of the Lord. Who is The Branch that shall build the temple of the Lord, and bear the glory, and be a priest and rule upon his throne?

Prophecies in Isaiah, Chapter, 11, Verses 1 and 2, give us that information. In Verse 1 we are told, "And there shall come forth a rod out of the stem of Jesse, and a Branch shall grow out of his roots." It's important that I note here the fact that Jesse fathered King David. And in Verse 2, we are told, "And the spirit of the LORD shall rest upon him, the spirit of wisdom and understanding, the spirit of counsel and might, the spirit of knowledge and of the fear of the LORD."

Jesus fulfilled those Isaiah, Chapter 11, prophecies, through Verses in Lections 2 and 8. In Verse 1 of Lection 2 we are told, "AND in the sixth month the angel Gabriel was sent from God, unto a city of Galilee, named Nazareth, to a virgin espoused to a man whose name was *Joseph, of the house of David*; and the virgin's name was Mary." The fulfilling part of that Verse is the fact that we are told Joseph, Jesus' father, had been from the house of David.

And in Verse 2 of Lection 8 we are told, "And Jesus, when he was baptized, went up straightway out of the water; and, lo, the heavens were opened unto him, and a bright cloud stood over him, and from behind the cloud Twelve Rays of light, and thence in the form of a Dove, the Spirit of God descending and lighting upon him. And, lo, a voice from heaven saying, This is my beloved Son, in whom I am well pleased; this day have I begotten thee" That Verse tells us the Lord told Jesus He had begotten him, and thus being, it

8

fulfilled Verse 2, of Isaiah, Chapter 11, which stated, "the spirit of the LORD shall rest upon him, the spirit of wisdom and understanding, the spirit of counsel and might, the spirit of knowledge and of the fear of the LORD."

Verse 15 of Zechariah, Chapter 6, told us, "And they that are far off shall come and build in the temple of the LORD, and ye shall know that the LORD of hosts hath sent me unto you." Jesus, sent by "the LORD of hosts," did build in the temple, as is made clear in today's reading of Jesus' Gospel, Lection 44, and specifically in Verses 4 and 5.

Verse 4 tells us, "All truth is in God, and I bear witness unto the truth. I am the true Rock, and on this Rock do I build my Church, and the gates of Hades shall not prevail against it, and out of this Rock shall flow rivers of living water to give life to the peoples of the earth," and Verse 5 states, "Ye are my chosen twelve. In me, the Head and Corner stone, are the twelve foundations of my house builded on the rock, and on you in me shall my Church be built, and in truth and righteousness shall my Church be established."

Earlier I stated that Verse 4 of Zechariah, Chapter 5, tells us the angel told Zechariah, "I will bring it forth, saith the LORD of hosts, and it shall enter into the house of him that sweareth falsely by my name," and I mentioned that the New Testament does not contain all the important doctrine that Jesus preached. Further to that I should also share with you that New Testament contains many partial accountings of lessons Jesus taught, and because they are partial, they convey a message that He did not intend. I can also share with you: Jesus knew it would happen.

Jesus told his chosen Twelve in Lection 44, Verse 7, "But there shall arise after you, men of perverse minds who shall through ignorance or through craft, suppress many things which I have spoken unto you, and lay to me things which I never taught, sowing tares among the good wheat which I have given you to sow in the world."

Those who had the authority, certainly employed craft when making changes to the doctrine Jesus preached, for when they recorded only part of a lesson Jesus taught, it conveyed a message Jesus did not intend. However, the message conveyed, certainly suited the needs and traditions of the authors. You may recall that I mentioned earlier: Jesus said children of the wicked one would be responsible; and Apostle Peter said children of the wicked were responsible.

Speaking about children of the wicked one, Pharisee Saul/Paul makes his first appearance in the New Testament in the Book of Acts, and his epistles make up 66% of the New Testament. As I have made clear in other homilies, Pharisee Saul/Paul preached doctrine contrary to that of Jesus and prophets before Him, and he did such to maintain the integrity of the blood covenant of Exodus 24, and the blood sacrifice laws of Exodus, Chapter 29.

Due to the fact Pharisee Saul/Paul, falsely preached doctrine that stated Jesus' crucifixion had been a blood sacrifice, to redeem mankind from their sin, he successfully protected the revered Hebrew blood covenant, and blood sacrifice laws, and thus being, the stigma of the blood sacrifice permeates almost the entire New Testament.

With that in mind, Jesus told His chosen Twelve, in Verse 12, within Lection 44, of His Gospel recorded by Apostle John, "Woe is the time when the spirit of the world entereth into the Church, and my doctrines and precepts are made void through the corruption of men and of women. Woe is the world when the Light is hidden. Woe is the world when these things shall be," and then in Verse 13, "Jesus lifted his voice and said, I thank thee, O most righteous Parent, Creator of Heaven and Earth, that though these things are

10

hidden from the wise and the prudent, they are nevertheless revealed unto babes."

Who are the babes? They are those who seek truth. And who are the wise and prudent? They are those who believe the Bible is true as written. Jesus told His chosen Twelve in Verse 8 of Lection 44, "Then shall the truth of God endure the contradiction of sinners, for thus it hath been, and thus it will be. But the time cometh when the things which they have hidden shall be revealed and made known, and the truth shall make free those which were bound." Brothers and Sisters in Christ, I firmly believe that time which Jesus spoke of in Verse 8, has arrived, for there are many who, in this electronic age of information sharing, are doing as I.

Brothers and Sisters, I again humbly beseech you to please become a warrior for God and Jesus, and share Their Truths with others, as I have shared with you.

Chapter 3

Homily: A discussion of the messages conveyed in Leviticus 1, as they apply other books within the Old Testament, and to lessons Jesus taught in His Gospel, and lessons Apostle Peter preached in The Clementine Homilies.

Today's reading of Leviticus, Chapter 1, Verses 1 thru 9, is a rehash of the blood covenant within Exodus, Chapter 24, and the rituals revolving around the blood sacrifice laws given in Exodus, Chapter 29. I have stated often in my homilies over the past couple of years that the blood sacrifice laws are of men, and not of God, and I have referenced Verses which prove that fact, within Jesus' Gospel recorded by Apostle John, and within the Old Testament.

Today's reading of the Gospel of the Holy Twelve, Lection 28, Verses 1 thru 12, contained one such Verse wherein Jesus denounced the bloody sacrifices of the law:

3. Ye believe that Moses indeed commanded such creatures to be slain and offered in sacrifice and eaten, and so do ye in the Temple, but behold a greater than Moses is herein and he cometh to put away the bloody sacrifices of the law, and the feasts on them, and to restore to you the pure oblation and unbloody sacrifice as in the beginning, even the grains and fruits of the earth.

There is yet another very important ancient biblical writing that confirms Jesus preached against the blood covenant of Exodus 24, and the blood sacrifice rituals and laws of Exodus 29. That ancient writing is known as The Clementine Homilies. The Clementine Homilies are of Clement of Rome, a Church Father who had been personally trained in Jesus' Doctrine by Apostle Peter, and Peter appointed him to be a Church Father. In addition to an epistle from Apostle Peter, to Jesus' brother, Apostle

James, and an epistle from Clement to James, The Clementine Homilies contains a record of the doctrine Apostle Peter preached.

There is a great significance to the fact it contains a record of the doctrine Peter preached. Why is that of importance? The messages of the lessons Peter preached, mirror the messages of the lessons Jesus preached in the Gospel of the Holy Twelve. Even more important: The Clementine Homilies is the fourth resource that, when combined with the other three: the Gospel of the Holy Twelve; and the King James and Catholic Bibles, together, prove beyond any shadow of a doubt whatsoever, Jesus did in fact preach against the bloody sacrifices of the law, and they also prove the Old and New Testaments of the King James and Catholic Bibles, contain deceit.

Being I have shared, over the past couple of years, many Verses in which Jesus preached against the bloody sacrifices of the law, I will share a lesson from The Clementine Homilies, in which Peter did likewise. But first, I want to share with you the fact that The Clementine Homilies reveals Apostle Peter had an antagonist, Simon Magnus. Simon appeared in the cities wherein Peter preached His Master's Doctrine, and because Simon had an informant in Peter's group, there were times he preceded Peter by a few days.

When Simon preceded Peter in a city, he attempted to incite the people against him, but Peter always overcame the trouble Simon brewed, and I firmly believe he did so thru the fact that he performed miraculous healings after he preached, as did his Master. Simon had been a magician, and it is recorded that he could levitate, but he could not perform the healings as did Peter.

Now that you have a bit of a history regarding Simon Magnus, I will share a section within The Clementine Homilies, wherein Apostle Peter preached against the blood sacrifice. Peter met with Simon in Tyre, a port in southern Lebanon on the Mediterranean Sea, and in Chapter III of Homily VII, Peter said,

"Now I have been told, that after he had [blood] sacrificed an ox he feasted you in the middle of the forum, and when you partook of meat offered to idols, you became servants to the prince of evil, in like manner, if you cease from these things, and flee for refuge to God through the good Prince of His right hand [Jesus], honouring Him without [blood] sacrifices, by doing whatsoever He wills, know of a truth that not only will your bodies be healed, but your souls also will become healthy."

When studying The Clementine Homilies, every time I read an accounting of Simon Magnus' behavior, I automatically equated it to being the same as that of Pharisee Saul, and wondered if Simon Magnus and Pharisee Saul were one in the same. When studying certain parts of 'The Catholic Encyclopedia,' I uncovered very revealing information regarding Simon Magnus, and Pharisee Saul / apostle to the Gentiles, Paul – it stated, "Simon Magnus never existed; it is a nickname for St. Paul."

Those who are staunch defenders of Paul, steadfastly stand by 2 Peter 3:15, that is within the New Testament, which states, "And account that the longsuffering of our Lord is salvation; even as our beloved brother Paul also according to the wisdom given unto him hath written unto you;"

The information I shared with you regarding Apostle Peter, and his confrontations with Simon Magnus, who is Pharisee Saul, a/k/a apostle to the Gentiles, Paul, crystallizes the fact Peter would not have identified Paul, in Verse 15, as being a beloved brother. Being such, it is deceitful information implanted in Peter's epistle, by those who had the authority to do such, and it is clear they did so to further protect the creation of apostle to the Gentiles, Paul, in a well crafted effort to maintain the integrity of the

14

longstanding and revered blood covenant of Exodus 24, and the blood sacrifice laws of Exodus 29.

I want to share a very important statement Clement of Rome wrote in his Homilies, "There is a certain great difference between truth and custom. For truth is found when it is honestly sought; but custom, whatsoever be the character of the custom received, whether true or false, is strengthened by itself without the exercise of judgment; and he who has received it is neither pleased with it as being true, nor grieved with it as false. For such an one has believed not by judgment, but by prejudice, resting his own hope on the opinion of those who have lived before him on a mere peradventure. And it is not easy to cast off the ancestral garment, though it be shown to himself to be wholly foolish and ridiculous."

Brothers and Sisters in Christ, there are many Christians, who vehemently defend their Bible as being true as written, and they absolutely refuse to even look at anything which could contradict their revered beliefs, or as Clement of Rome stated: they refuse to remove the ancestral garment.

However, there are many Christians who will listen to and want to learn God's and His Son's truths. As those who preached God's and His Son's truths before us, we do not know who those people will be, until we attempt to share, and as a modern day disciple of Jesus, I'd like you to please take this into consideration:

- prophets before Jesus preached doctrine that contradicted the revered blood covenant and blood sacrifices, for which all were reviled, and some were slain, as Jesus stated in Lection 52, Verse 6; and
- Jesus preached against the revered blood covenant and blood sacrifices, for which He suffered horrible beatings and crucifixion; and

15

- His Apostles preached against the revered blood covenant and blood sacrifices, for which they were reviled and slain; and

- Jesus' followers after His resurrection preached against the revered blood covenant and blood sacrifices, for which some were reviled, while others were slain; and
- those trained in Jesus' Doctrine, who were initiated into the Christhood, preached against the revered blood covenant and blood sacrifices, for which some were reviled, and others were slain.

Those Disciples of Christ knew they were tempting the wrath of those who fought to suppress that which Jesus had taught, and in spite of that knowledge, still preached His Doctrine. Brothers and Sisters, in my humble opinion, they were true warriors for God and Jesus, for they willingly put life and limb on the line.

In this day and age, most of us, unless we live in a country wherein Christians are severely persecuted, have little to fear by preaching God's and His Son's truth, which is revealed in the Gospel of the Holy Twelve and The Clementine Homilies. We can certainly expect to be ridiculed by those who persist in standing behind the Bible as it is written, but ridicule is nothing, when it is compared to that which prophets, Jesus, and His disciples had to endure.

Jesus gave this parable in Lection 57, Verse 5, "How think ye? if a man have a hundred sheep, and one of them be gone astray, doth he not leave the ninety and nine and go into the mountains and seek that which is gone astray? And if so be that he find it, verily I say unto you, he rejoiceth more over that sheep than over the ninety and nine which went not astray."

Brothers and Sisters in Christ, even if you bring only one soul to God's and His Son's Truths, what a wonderful act of love you have given. I again urge you to become a staunch warrior for God and His Son. I urge you with all my heart, soul and mind, to preach Their truths that I share with you. Don't be afraid – wearing the full armor of God, I will support you should you encounter an adversary who appears to be willing to listen, but is extremely difficult to convince

Chapter 4

Homily: A discussion of the messages conveyed in Amos 5, as they apply other books within the Old Testament, and to lessons Jesus and Apostle Peter taught.

Brothers and Sisters in Christ, there are a couple of Verses within today's reading of the Old Testament, Amos, Chapter 5 that I want to address, the first being Verse 10, wherein we are told, "They hate him that rebuketh in the gate, and they abhor him that speaketh uprightly." This Verse speaks well of Jesus, for He certainly rebuked within the gate.

What did he rebuke? He rebuked the daily blood sacrifices carried out within the temple for the atonement of sin, and the Pharisees, priests and scribes certainly hated him for speaking uprightly against the daily blood sacrifice, which ultimately led to His crucifixion.

In Verse 11 we were told, "Forasmuch therefore as your treading is upon the poor, and ye take from him burdens of wheat:" and Verse 12 stated: "For I know your manifold transgressions and your mighty sins: they afflict the just, they take a bribe, and they turn aside the poor in the gate from their right." These Verses tie very well with a parable in Jesus' Gospel recorded by Apostle John, which is in Lection 47, Verses 11 thru 14.

Those Verses tell us a beggar named Lazarus, who full of sores, laid at a rich man's gate, wanting to be fed, however, the rich man ignored him. When Lazarus died, angels carried him unto Abraham's bosom, and when the rich man died, he was buried with great pomp. But the rich man ended up in Hades, and while being in torments he saw Abraham afar off, with the beggar Lazarus, in his bosom.

The rich man cried out to Abraham for mercy, and asked him to send Lazarus that he may have a little water to cool his tongue. Abraham then told the rich man, remember how you received good things in your lifetime, while Lazarus received evil things; but see now how he is comforted, and you are tormented. Then he told the rich man: these are the changes of life for the perfecting of souls.

Jesus taught often throughout His Gospel recorded by Apostle John, that souls experience many lifetimes to achieve the purification required to enter into the Kingdom of Heaven, and he also taught that as you sow in this lifetime, so shall ye reap in the next. Further to His statement, "as you sow so shall you reap," Jesus also taught that God will forgive sins of those who repent and amend their ways, and if they forsake the sin, they are loosed from it.

However, Jesus added: even though the sin is forgiven, penance must still be paid, for God is not mocked. And in addition to that, Jesus taught: if a soul commits a sin again, which had been forgiven, the soul will be bound to it, and would have been better off had it not asked for forgiveness to begin with.

Today's reading of Jesus' Gospel also had some verses that I want to further address, and one of them is Verse 2, when Jesus told some of His stonemason disciples who were repairing the temple, "Yea, it is beautiful, and well wrought are the stones, but the time cometh when not one stone shall be left on another, for the enemy shall overthrow both the city and the Temple." As Jesus foretold of the destruction, so does the Book of Daniel herald the destruction of the city and the temple.

Daniel, Chapter 8, Verse 11 states, "Yea, he magnified himself even to the prince of the host, and by him the daily sacrifice was taken away, and the place of his sanctuary was cast down," and Chapter 9, Verse 26 tells us, "And after threescore and two weeks shall Messiah be cut off, but not for himself: and the people of the prince that shall come shall destroy the city and the sanctuary." The pertinent sections of these Verses, as they apply to Jesus' statement in Verse 2 of his Gospel, are as follows: in Daniel 8:11, "the place of his sanctuary was cast down;" and in Daniel 9:26, "the people of the prince that shall come shall destroy the city and the sanctuary."

Those two statements coincide perfectly with Jesus' statement in Verse 2 of His Gospel, "the enemy shall overthrow both the city and the Temple." Both Daniel 8:11, and Daniel 9:26 mentioned "the prince," and Verse 25, of Daniel, Chapter 9, tells us who the prince is, "to build Jerusalem unto the Messiah the Prince." Now that we have that bit of information, we still need to know who the people of the prince are, that are mentioned in Daniel 9:26, and that answer is provided to us through two resources: historical documents, and Jesus' Gospel.

Jesus told us in today's reading of his Gospel, in Verse 7, "Again it is written, From the rising of the sun unto the setting of the same, my Name shall be great among the Gentiles, and incense with a pure Offering shall be offered unto me." Further to Verse 7, Jesus gave a prophecy in Lection 89, Verse 9, which told us, "And yet another shall arise and he shall teach many things which I have taught you already, and he shall spread the Gospel among the Gentiles with great zeal."

The "another" whom Jesus declared would arise and teach many things which He had already taught His disciples, had been Pharisee Saul a/k/a Simon Magnus, who became known as apostle to the Gentiles, Paul. However, as I have shared in other homilies, in addition to preaching doctrine that Jesus had taught, Paul also taught doctrine in Jesus' Name that He did not teach. And Jesus made it clear He knew that would happen when He stated in His prophecy, "he shall teach many things which I have taught you already;" He did not state He would teach everything He had taught them already.

20

What did Saul/Paul teach in his epistles, that Jesus and His Apostles and those who were initiated into the Christhood, did not teach? Saul/Paul declared in his epistles, Jesus' crucifixion, had been a blood sacrifice, to redeem mankind from their sin. Jesus taught, "No blood offering, of beast or bird, or man, can take away sin, for how can the conscience be purged from sin by the shedding of innocent blood? Nay, it will increase the condemnation. The priests indeed receive such offering as a reconciliation of the worshippers for the trespasses against the law of Moses, but for sins against the Law of God there can be no remission, save by repentance and amendment."

History makes clear two versions of Christianity were taught to the Romans: 1 – the doctrine Jesus had given, which was preached by those initiated into the Christhood, within the group known as the Jewish Christian Movement; and the 2nd had been the doctrine preached by Saul/Paul, who had not been initiated into the Christhood.

The lessons taught by those two groups to Romans throughout the Roman Empire, resulted in the fulfillment of Jesus' prophecy in Verse 7 of today's reading, "my Name shall be great among the Gentiles, and incense with a pure Offering shall be offered unto me." Through the efforts of those two groups, the Jewish Christian Movement, and Pauline Christianity, the Romans became the people of the prince, as identified in Daniel 9:26, and in 70 A.D., historical documents reveal that the Romans destroyed Jerusalem, and the Temple.

The statement Jesus made in Verse 8 of today's reading, "Know ye not what is written? Obedience is better than sacrifice and to hearken than the fat of rams. I, the Lord, am weary of your burnt offerings, and vain oblations, your hands are full of blood," ties directly with statements the Lord made to Isaiah, in Chapter 1, Verses 11 and 12, which declare, "To what purpose is the multitude of your sacrifices unto me? saith the LORD: I am full of the burnt offerings of rams, and the fat of fed beasts; and I delight not in the blood of bullocks, or of lambs, or of he goats. When ye come to appear before me, who hath required this at your hand, to tread my courts?"

Brothers and Sisters, you are Christ's disciples, and I ask you to take up His Cross and become a warrior for Him and His Father; I ask you to trumpet Their Truths that I share with you, to as many people as you can. Fear not those who choose to rebuke you, for they are the loser, and you are the winner, for you did your best to share God's and Jesus' Truths with them.

Think about this: every time you share God's and His Son's Truths with a fellow Christian, it is an act of unselfish love, and that fact, in-and-of-itself, is very important; Why? Jesus told His disciples in Lection 69, Verse 6, "Believe ye not that any man is wholly without error, for even among the prophets, and those who have keen initiated into the Christhood, the word of error has been found. But there are a multitude of error which are covered by love." Cover multitudes of error, thru love for your fellow Christians, and teach them, thru love, that which is the true Word of God, and the true Doctrine of His Son, Jesus.

Chapter 5

Homily: A discussion of: Psalms 22 prophecies which Jesus fulfilled; and why certain crucial lessons Jesus preached are not in the New Testament.

Brothers and Sisters in Christ, today's reading of Psalms 22, Verses 1 through 16, contains prophecies which Jesus fulfilled that I want to bring to your attention; the first being in Verse 7, which states, "All they that see me laugh me to scorn," and Jesus fulfilled that prophecy in Lection 82, through Verses 15 and 18. The first fulfillment, which is in Verse 15, states, "one of the malefactors which were hanged railed on him," and the second in Verse 18 tells us, "Likewise also the chief priests mocking him."

The 2nd prophecy in Verse 8 of Psalms 22, declares, "He trusted on the LORD that he would deliver him: let him deliver him," and Jesus fulfilled that prophecy in Lection 82, Verse 15, when a malefactor being crucified next to Him, said, "If thou be the Christ, save thy self and us." Verse 15 of Lection 82 also fulfilled the Psalms 22, Verse 8 prophecy, when the scribes and elders said, "If he be the King of Israel, let him now come down from the cross," which they finished by saying, "He trusted in God, let Him deliver him now."

Psalms 22, Verse 14 prophesied, "I am poured out like water," and Verse 31 of Lection 82, fulfilled that prophecy through this part, "forthwith came there out blood and water." And there is one more prophecy in today's reading of Psalms 22, which is in Verse 16, "they pierced my hands and my feet." Jesus' fulfillment of that prophecy is recorded within Verse 4 of Lection 87 - For Thomas, called Didymus, had said unto them, Except I shall see in his hands the print of the nails, I will not believe. Then saith Jesus to Thomas, Behold my hands, and my feet; reach hither thy hands, and be not faithless but believing.

23

Psalms 22 contains yet another prophecy Jesus fulfilled, although it had not been included in today's reading, and it is in Verse 18, which states, "They cast lots upon my vesture." Lection 82, Verse 12 fulfills that prophecy through this statement, "They parted my raiment among them, and for my vesture they did cast lots."

There are also Verses within today's reading of Jesus' Gospel that I would like to address, and the first is Verse 1, wherein it is stated, "THEN the same day at evening, being the first day of the week, when the doors were shut where the disciples were assembled for fear of the Jews."

Why would it be that Jesus' disciples would be afraid? Could it be they feared for their well being, due to the fact they taught and preached, as did Jesus, against the blood covenant of Exodus 24, and the blood sacrifice rituals and laws of Exodus 29, which resulted in the Jews demanding that the Romans crucify their Master?

I have stated in other homilies that important lessons Jesus taught are missing from the New Testament, and perhaps you have wondered how that could possibly be. Verse 6 of Lection 87, in today's reading provides a foundation to that answer. In Verse 6, Jesus told His disciples, "Peace be unto you, as Abba Amma hath sent me, even so send I you. And when he had said this he breathed on them and said unto them, Receive ye the Holy Ghost; preach the Gospel, and announce ye unto all nations; the resurrection of the Son of Man."

Jesus sent out His disciples to preach to the world His Gospel, while at the same time announcing to all nations His resurrection, which absolutely proved Him to be the Son of God. The disciples Jesus sent out, were of a group that became known as the Jewish Christian Movement, which was one of three major groups of Christianity that evolved after Jesus' crucifixion. Another of the three

24

groups that evolved became known as Pauline Christianity, and the third became known as Gnostic Christianity.

A serious power struggle evolved between the leader of the Jewish Christian Movement, Apostle Peter, and the leader of Pauline Christianity, Pharisee Saul, a.k.a. Simon Magnus, a.k.a. apostle to the Gentiles, Paul, and it boiled down to the need to gain and maintain control of the Church Jesus had established on the Rock through His chosen Twelve.

Why would that have been? Jesus, throughout His Gospel recorded by Apostle John, had preached against the blood covenant of Exodus 24, and the blood rituals and sacrifices of Exodus 29, Verses 10 through 42, which were revered and long-standing Hebrew laws, and the Jewish religious leaders wanted to maintain the integrity of those revered laws.

Is there biblical evidence which proves my statement to be fact? The answer is yes, and it is in Verses within Lection 75 and 76. Verse 6 of Lection 75 tells us Judas said to Jesus at the Last Paschal Supper, "Master, behold the unleaven bread, the mingled wine and the oil and the herbs, but where is the lamb that Moses commanded? (*for Judas had bought the lamb, but Iesus had forbidden that it should be killed*)."

Then Verses 27 and 28 of Lection 76 tell us Judas went to the house of Caiaphas, a high priest, and said, "Behold he [Jesus] has celebrated the Passover within the gates with the Mazza in place of the lamb. I indeed bought a lamb, but he forbade that it should be killed, and lo, the man of whom I bought it is witness. And Caiaphas rent his clothes and said, Truly this is a Passover of the law of Moses. He hath done the deed which is worthy of death, for it is a weighty transgression of the law. What need of further witness?"

Jesus had preached against the bloody sacrifices of the law, but that did not violate Hebrew Law. However, when He refused to allow the Passover lamb to be slaughtered in accordance with Moses' Passover Law, and celebrated Passover with Mazza instead, the Jews then had the means by which they could demand that Jesus be put to death. But what does this have to do with the struggle between Apostle Peter and Pharisee Saul/Paul to gain control of Jesus' Church?

History makes it very clear Pharisee Saul hunted, persecuted and was directly responsible for the imprisonment and or deaths of many members of the Jewish Christian Movement, and he did so because they believed in doctrine Jesus taught, which eliminated the revered blood covenant, and blood sacrifice rituals and laws of Exodus. Further to that, Jewish religious leaders had to accept the fact that being Jesus' resurrection proved Him to be the Son of God, the Jewish Christian Movement would continue to flourish.

That fact, in and of itself, had to be a huge problem for the hard-line Jewish religious leaders who fiercely protected traditional Hebrew Law. Why? As the Jewish Christian Movement gained in size and strength, the longstanding and revered blood covenant and blood sacrifice laws could be placed in jeopardy. With that possibility facing them, what could the Jewish religious leaders do to stave off such a threat to their longstanding traditions? Pharisee Saul/Paul provided that answer thru the fact that he preached Jesus' crucifixion had been a blood sacrifice to redeem mankind from their sin, which melded very well with the blood sacrifice laws of Exodus 29, for the atonement of sin.

History tells us Apostle Peter had recorded his Master's Doctrine, and history also tells us that Roman Emperor Constantine wanted to bring peace between the various religious factions throughout the Roman Empire, and decided to attempt to do so by unifying church doctrine. To that end, Constantine convened and presided over the First Council of Nicea 325 A.D.

After the Council adjourned, history tells us Constantine ordered all of the religious writings that contained doctrine that had not been authorized by the Council, to be destroyed. Thankfully, the Apostles agreed with Apostle John, to hide in a safe place, Jesus' Gospel that John had written.

Historical evidence clearly points to the fact that Constantine had learned in early in his political career, that converting to Christianity could be advantageous to fulfilling his political goals. History also makes clear Orthodox Nicene Bishops of the Catholic Church, desired to gain power by uniting with Roman hierarchy. Keeping those realities in mind, history reveals the fact those Bishops did unite with Constantine to influence the vote of those who attended the First Council of Nicaea 325 AD, to adopt the doctrine preached by Pharisee Saul/Paul, over that which had been preached by those within the Jewish Christian Movement.

The end result: after the Council adjourned, those who continued to believe in the doctrine of the Jewish Christian movement, were deemed to be heretics, and excommunicated from the church. Further, Constantine provided funding to the Catholic Church to write 50 Bibles, which gave the Church the incredible opportunity to create doctrine as they saw fit. Sadly, due to that fact, much of the doctrine Jesus gave to mankind that is crucial to a sole's salvation, is missing from the New Testament, and instead one finds the gift of salvation, preached by Pharisee Saul/Paul.

In Verse nine of Lection 87, Jesus said, "Lo, I have given my body and my blood to be offered on the Cross, for the redemption of the world from the sin against love, and from the bloody sacrifices and feasts of the past," and that

27

statement fulfills the Daniel 8:11 and 9:27 prophecies, wherein we are told that the Messiah would end the daily sacrifice.

Then in Verse 10 of today's reading, Jesus said, "And ye shall offer the Bread of life, and the Wine of salvation, for a pure Oblation with incense, as it is written of me, and ye shall eat and drink thereof for a memorial, that I have delivered all who believe in me from the ancient bondage of your ancestors." What did Jesus mean when he stated, "I have delivered all who believe in me from the ancient bondage of your ancestors?" He had been referring directly to the bondage of the blood covenant of Exodus 24, and of the blood sacrifice rituals and laws of Exodus 29.

And that fact is made very clear by His statement in Verse 11, "For they, making a god of their belly, sacrificed unto their god the innocent creatures of the earth, in place of the carnal nature within themselves." Jesus came to end the blood sacrifices that were carried out in the temple for the atonement of sin, and thus being, God would not have sent His Son to be a blood sacrifice to redeem mankind from their sin. On the other hand, God would have sent His Son to reestablish the steps that Holy Spirit had originally given to mankind, to earn their salvation, and Jesus did exactly that.

Brothers and Sisters, Jesus in His Sermon on the Mount, said, "Behold One greater than Moses is here, and he [Jesus] will give you the higher law, even the perfect Law, and this Law shall ye obey. Whosoever therefore shall break one of these commandments which he [Jesus] shall give, and shall teach men so, they shall be called the least in the kingdom; but whosoever shall do, and teach them, the same shall be called great in the kingdom of Heaven."

Brothers and Sisters in Christ, I once again ask you to take up Jesus' Cross, and be a warrior for Him and His Father, and share with any and all who will listen, the lessons of

28

Their Truths that I share with you. I know that rejection can be difficult for some to handle, but if rejection is taken with a positive attitude, by knowing within one's heart, that thru love one had attempted to help a fellow Christian, by sharing with them the truth about God's steps to salvation that have been hidden from them, then rejection takes on a whole different meaning. Fear not the rejection, and do that which is difficult, and revel in knowing that you shall be called great in the kingdom of Heaven.

Chapter 6

Homily: How prophecies which Jesus fulfilled, apply in our daily lives.

Brothers and Sisters in Christ, I want to expound upon a few of the Old Testament prophecies Jesus fulfilled, and the first is Psalms, Chapter 41, Verse 9, wherein the prophecy stated, "hath lifted up his heel against me." The person who lifted up his heel against Jesus, had been Judas, for he is the one who betrayed Jesus with a kiss, as it is stated in Lection 78, Verse 5, "Is it with a kiss that thou betrayest the Son of man."

In addition, I want to bring to your attention the fact that I mentioned Judas in the opening prayers as being among Jesus' Twelve Apostles, but I also made it obvious that Judas had not been one of them, which directly contradicts the New Testaments of the King James and Catholic Bibles.

The next prophecies are within Isaiah 53, Verses 5 and 6 and 12. In Verse 5 it is stated, "He was wounded for our transgressions, and bruised for our iniquities," and Verse 6 tells us, "the LORD hath laid on him the iniquity of us all." And then in Verse 12 we were told, "he bare the sin of many, and made intercession for the transgressors." These are very important prophecies, but who exactly, are they referring to?

I'll answer that question by first sharing with you the Daniel 9:27 prophecy, which Jesus fulfilled, "in the midst of the week he shall cause the sacrifice and the oblation to cease," and that prophecy ties directly with the Daniel 8:11 prophecy, which states, "he magnified himself even to the prince of the host, and by him the daily sacrifice was taken away,"

The Daniel 9:25 prophecy tells us, "Know therefore and understand, that from the going forth of the commandment to restore and to build Jerusalem unto the Messiah the Prince shall be seven weeks, and threescore and two weeks." This prophecy provides several important pieces of information, one of which tells the reader "Messiah is the Prince," who had been identified in Daniel 8:11, as the "prince of the host."

The Daniel 9:25 prophecy also tells us, "from the going forth of the commandment to restore and to build Jerusalem." That statement should generate a couple of questions in our minds: 1 – who gave the commandment, and 2 - when was it given? That answer is provided in Ezra, Chapter 7, Verses 12 and 13, wherein King Artaxerxes told the Jews, "I make a decree, that all they of the people of Israel, which are minded of their own freewill to go up to Jerusalem." A decree is defined as being "A legally binding command."

Then in Verse 21, King Artaxerxes stated, "I Artaxerxes the king, do make a decree to all the treasurers which are beyond the river, that whatsoever Ezra the priest, the scribe of the law of the God of heaven, shall require of you, it be done speedily." What did the law of the God of Heaven require of the Jews? That answer was given in Daniel 9:25, "restore and to build Jerusalem unto the Messiah the Prince," and in Ezra, Chapter 7, Verse 21, King Artaxerxes provided the funds the Jews needed to "restore and to build Jerusalem unto the Messiah the Prince."

The only piece of information not given in the Old Testament is when King Artaxerxes issued that decree, and fortunately archeologists uncovered a stone tablet containing information that confirmed King Artaxerxes' decree, as well the date he issued it, which had been in 457 BC.

However, we still need another bit of information to calculate the timing of the events prophesied in Daniel 9:24-27 prophecies, and that is: what is a week equal to in Biblical prophecy? We can find that answer in the Books of Ezekiel and Numbers.

First is this section of Ezekiel 4:6, "thou shalt bear the iniquity of the house of Judah forty days: I have appointed thee each day for a year," and 2nd, this section of Numbers 14:34, "After the number of the days in which ye searched the land, even forty days, each day for a year." Those Verse sections make it clear that one day in Biblical prophecy is equal to one year.

Now that we are armed with all this information, we can calculate the timing in prophecy given in the Daniel 9:24 - 27 prophecies, which I have done, and the timing in prophecy reveals Jesus had been crucified exactly in the time frame as had been foretold in Daniel 9:27 prophecy, "in the midst of the week."

By the way, I think it is apropos that I share with you the fact that there is a Rabbinic Curse that addresses those prophecies, and it states: "May the bones of the hands and the bones of the fingers decay and decompose, of him who turns the pages of the book of Daniel, to find out the time of Daniel 9:24-27, and may his memory rot from off the face of the earth forever" If you wish to look it up, you will find it in Talmudic Law, page 978, Section 2, Line 28.

That's a very serious curse, and being I did calculate those times given in prophecy, I totally understand why the Jewish religious leaders chose to issue such a curse, for if one applies the information as given in the prophecies, they will come to this conclusion: the Jewish religion no longer exists.

The Daniel 9:24 prophecy states, "Seventy weeks are determined upon thy people and upon thy holy city, to

32

finish the transgression, and to make an end of sins, and to make reconciliation for iniquity." Sections of the Daniel 9:24 prophecy tie directly with the Isaiah, Chapter 53 prophecies that are in Verses 5 and 6 and 12; for instance, this section of Daniel 9:24, "to finish the transgression," ties with this section of Isaiah 53, Verse 5, "wounded for our transgressions," and this section of Daniel 9:24 states, "to make reconciliation for iniquity," which ties with this section of Isaiah 53, Verse 6, "the LORD hath laid on him the iniquity of us all," and this section of Daniel 9:24, "and to make an end of sins," ties with this section of Verse 12, "he bare the sin of many."

Now that we can see how the prophecies within Daniel, Chapter 9, tie with the prophecies in Isaiah, Chapter 53, it makes clear the transgressions, sins and iniquities that were addressed in Isaiah, Chapter 53, Verses 5 and 6 and 12, and again in Daniel 9:24, were the daily sacrifice; why? The Messiah came to end them, as it was foretold in the Daniel 8:11 and 9:27 prophecies.

Further confirmation to that fact are the lessons that Jesus preached often in the Gospel of the Holy Twelve, in which He told His chosen Twelve, and His followers: He came to end the blood sacrifices of the law, and the law He addressed each and every time, had been the blood covenant instituted by Moses, in Exodus 24, and the blood sacrifice rituals and laws within Exodus 29.

The lessons I have mentioned in this homily are just a few of the many which make it crystal clear the sin Jesus came to end, the transgression He came to end, the iniquity He came to end, was the daily sacrifice carried out by the Jews within the Temple, and not to redeem all of mankind from their sins.

In addition, Jesus made it clear whom He came to redeem, in Matthew, Chapter 15, Verse 24 of the King James Bible, KJV, when He said, "But he answered and said, I am not sent but unto the lost sheep of the house of Israel." Further to that statement, Jesus did preach the doctrine which mankind must obey to earn salvation, and through the many lessons He preached, He made it crystal clear: salvation is earned, and is not a gift.

Chapter 7

Homily: A discussion of the Lords condemnation of the blood sacrifice in Isaiah 1, as it applies to Jesus' Gospel recorded by Apostle John.

Brothers and Sisters in Christ, today's reading of Isaiah, Chapter 1, contains a few Verses that I wish to discuss, the first being this part of Verse 2, "the LORD hath spoken, I have nourished and brought up children, and they have rebelled against me." Who are the children the Lord told Isaiah that rebelled against him? They are the Israelites.

The next is Verse 3, "The ox knoweth his owner, and the ass his master's crib: but Israel doth not know, my people doth not consider." The ox and the ass, respectively, know who their owner and master is, but the Lord is making it clear to Isaiah that the Israelites do not know Him, and do not take into consideration the commands which He had given them.

In Verse 4, the Lord openly states He is very upset with the Israelites when He tells Isaiah, "Ah sinful nation, a people laden with iniquity, a seed of evildoers, children that are corrupters: they have forsaken, they have provoked the Holy One of Israel unto anger, they are gone away backward."

Then the Lord, in Verses 5 through 9, continues to declare to Isaiah His displeasure with the Israelites, and then in Verse 10, He states to Isaiah, "Hear the word of the LORD," followed by this statement to Isaiah in Verse 11, "To what purpose is the multitude of your sacrifices unto me? saith the LORD: I am full of the burnt offerings of rams, and the fat of fed beasts; and I delight not in the blood of bullocks, or of lambs, or of he goats."

It is very clear that in Verse 11, the Lord is assuring Isaiah that burnt offerings of rams, and the fat of fed beasts, and the blood sacrifices of bullocks, lambs and he goats, is not something that pleases Him in any manner whatsoever. Then in Verse 12, the Lord asks Isaiah, "When ye come to appear before me, who hath required this at your hand?"

That is an extremely interesting question, "When ye come to appear before me, who hath required this at your hand?" Why is it so interesting? It's due to the fact that in Exodus, Chapter 29, Verses 10 through 42 make it clear the Lord gave Moses rituals, and laws, regarding blood sacrifices for the atonement of sin.

Could it be possible the Lord forgot that He gave Moses the rituals and laws to conduct blood sacrifices for the atonement of sin, in Chapter 29? I do not believe for one instant the Lord would forget such; so which is correct: the information in Exodus, Chapter 29, or the information contained in Isaiah, Chapter 1?

Further to that, in Verse 4 the Lord told this to Isaiah about the Israelites, "they are gone away backward," and that is a very significant statement, for it ties directly with something the Lord told the prophet, Jeremiah, in Chapter 7, Verses 22 through 24.

In Verse 22, the Lord told Jeremiah, "For I spake not unto your fathers, nor commanded them in the day that I brought them out of the land of Egypt, concerning burnt offerings or sacrifices," which ties directly with Isaiah, Chapter 1, Verse 11, which states, "To what purpose is the multitude of your sacrifices unto me? saith the LORD: I am full of the burnt offerings of rams, and the fat of fed beasts; and I delight not in the blood of bullocks, or of lambs, or of he goats."

Then, the Lord told Jeremiah in Verse 24, "But they hearkened not, nor inclined their ear, but walked in the counsels and in the imagination of their evil heart, and went backward, and not forward," which ties directly with this section of Isaiah, Chapter 1, Verse 4, that states, "they are gone away backward." How did the Israelites go backward? That answer is found in two biblical resources: Jeremiah, Chapter 7, Verse 23, and in Jesus' Gospel recorded by Apostle John, in Lection 51, Verse 15.

First I'll address Verse 23 of Jeremiah, Chapter 7, which states, "But this thing commanded I them, saying, Obey my voice, and I will be your God, and ye shall be my people: and walk ye in all the ways that I have commanded you, that it may be well unto you." and

Lection 51, Verse 15 tells us the exact commandment the Lord gave the Israelites, "As also Jeremiah bear witness when he saith, concerning blood offerings and sacrifices I the Lord God commanded none of these things in the day that ye came out of Egypt, but only this I commanded you to do, righteousness, walk in the ancient paths, do justice, love mercy, and walk humbly with thy God."

Further to that, it is written in Lection 28, Verse 3, "Ye believe that Moses indeed commanded such creatures to be slain and offered in sacrifice and eaten, and so do ye in the Temple, but behold a greater than Moses is herein and he cometh to put away the bloody sacrifices of the law, and the feasts on them, and to restore to you the pure oblation and unbloody sacrifice as in the beginning, even the grains and fruits of the earth."

And Lection 38, Verse 3 states, "God giveth the grains and the fruits of the earth for food: and for righteous man truly there is no other lawful sustenance for the body."

So how did the Israelites go backward? They went backward by creating their own laws, which were contrary to those originally given by God. God gave them a commandment that they must do righteousness, walk in the ancient paths, do justice, love mercy, and walk humbly with thy God, and he gave them the grains and fruits of the earth for food.

The Clementine Homilies, Homily III, Chapter XLVII [47], makes it clear that Moses never wrote the laws down which God had given to him, for he gave them verbally to 70 wise men, to be handed down to the generations. And Homily II, Chapter XXXVIII [38], crystallizes the fact that a while after Moses' death the law God gave to Moses, was written, and falsehoods were added to it which were contrary to the law of God. What laws were added? The cruel blood sacrifice laws for the atonement of sin, which had been done by the authors to suit their needs and traditions.

By the way, for the benefit of those who may not be familiar with The Clementine Homilies, they are of early Church Father, Clement of Rome, who had been personally trained by Apostle Peter in Jesus' Doctrine, and Peter personally appointed Clement to be a Church Father. The Homilies contain an epistle from Peter to James, Bishop of Jerusalem, and an epistle from Clement to Apostle James, as well as a record of the doctrine that Apostle Peter preached.

The major significance of The Clementine Homilies is this fact: the messages of the lessons that Apostle Peter preached, mirror the messages of the lessons Jesus taught as recorded by Apostle John, that are in the Gospel of the Holy Twelve.

There are also a few Verses within today's reading of the Gospel of the Holy Twelve, Lection 21, that I want to discuss, but first I want to bring to your attention the message conveyed in Verses 1 through 6. Those Verses tell us about an instance wherein Jesus and His disciples came upon a man who was beating his horse because it could not carry the very heavy load that had been placed upon it.

Jesus showed great compassion for the horse, and this is just one instance of many in His Gospel recorded by Apostle John, that he did such. Actually, in Lection 34, Verse 9, the Jews around Jesus, after seeing how He cared for a cat, said, "This man careth for all creatures, are they his brothers and sisters that he should love them? And he [Jesus] said unto them, Verily these are your fellow creatures of the great Household of God, yea, they are your brethren and sisters, having the same breath of life in the Eternal."

That statement Jesus made to the Jews around him, "they are your brethren and sisters, having the same breath of life in the Eternal," ties directly with Ecclesiastes, Chapter 3, Verse 19, which states, "For that which befalleth the sons of men befalleth beasts; even one thing befalleth them: as the one dieth, so dieth the other; yea, they have all one breath; so that a man hath no preeminence above a beast:"

In addition, in Lection 38, Verse 2, Jesus told His disciples, "Verily I say unto you, they who partake of benefits which are gotten by wronging one of God's creatures, cannot be righteous: nor can they touch holy things, or teach the mysteries of the kingdom, whose hands are stained with blood, or whose mouths are defiled with flesh."

Further to that, in Lection 21, Verse 6, after Jesus touched the horse and its wounds were healed, He told the man, "Go now thy way and strike it henceforth no more, if thou also desireth to find mercy." Wow, "if thou also desireth to find mercy." What a powerful statement that one should pay attention to, for it crystallizes this fact: any soul who is not merciful to God's creatures, or who wrongs His creatures…that soul shall find no mercy from God when it comes to His meting out the penance that must be paid, for the wrong, or wrongs that had been done.

Verse 8 within today's reading of Jesus' Gospel, also confirms that the bloody sacrifices of the law are not of God:

Verse 8. He also said, I am come to end the sacrifices and feasts of blood, and if ye cease not offering and eating of flesh and blood, the wrath of God shall not cease from you, even as it came to your fathers in the wilderness, who lusted for flesh, and they eat to their content, and were filled with rottenness, and the plague consumed them.

Wow, that's another very powerful statement one should pay close attention to: "I am come to end the sacrifices and feasts of blood, and if ye cease not offering and eating of flesh and blood, *the wrath of God shall not cease from you*."

Verse 9 contains a statement of great significance: Jesus told His chosen Twelve, "And I say unto you, Though ye be gathered together in my bosom, if ye keep not my commandments I will cast you forth. For if ye keep not the lesser mysteries, who shall give you the greater." What is so important about that statement?

The importance is bound by this fact: Pharisee Saul a.k.a. Simon Magnus a.k.a. apostle to the Gentiles, Paul, did not keep Jesus' commandments, and he did such by the fact that he hunted, and was directly responsible for the death of many of Jesus' followers. Think about this reality: Jesus told His chosen Twelve, who were good and just men given to him by his Father, that he would cast them forth if they did not keep His commandments. Being that is so, why would Jesus give Saul/Paul, who broke Jesus' Commandments, special treatment? While considering that information, keep in mind that Jesus vehemently preached against being a hypocrite. If Jesus gave Saul/Paul special treatment, wouldn't that be hypocritical?

The simple answer to that question is: He would not. Thus being, Pharisee Saul a.k.a. Simon Magnus a.k.a. apostle to the Gentiles, Paul, did not receive the greater mysteries, which would have been Jesus' Gospel, and that fact brings up a very important question...being Pharisee Saul/Paul did not have Jesus' Gospel, from whence did he receive the Gospel was he preaching, that he talked about so often in his epistles?

Brothers and Sisters in Christ, once again I humbly ask you to please be a warrior for God and Jesus, and share with all those whom you can, God's and Jesus' truths that I share with you. I make this request at the conclusion of each and every worship service, for it is extremely important. So many Christians believe Christ died on the cross as a blood sacrifice to redeem them from their sins, and those who have studied Jesus' Gospel recorded by Apostle John, and The Clementine Homilies, know, beyond a shadow of a doubt, that Jesus did *not* die on the cross to redeem all of mankind from their sins, as the false apostle, Paul, preached.

Jesus foretold to His chosen Twelve, the children of the wicked one would be responsible for sowing tears in the good wheat that he had given them to sow in the world, and Apostle Peter confirmed it was happening, even during his time, and he did so in Chapter II, of his epistle to Apostle James, that is within The Clementine Homilies.

Brothers and Sisters, who benefits most by the fact that so many Christians believe false doctrine? It is the wicked one! Once again I ask you to please help me and all the others who are dedicated warriors to God and His Son, Jesus: please help us thwart the efforts of the wicked one, and share the Truths Jesus gave us. I assure you, based upon Jesus' teachings, your rewards will be great.

Chapter 8

Homily: A discussion of Isaiah 53 prophesies Jesus fulfilled, and other Old Testament prophecies that tie with Isaiah 53, which negate the grace and salvation preached by Pharisee Saul/Paul.

Brothers and Sisters, today's reading of Isaiah, Chapter 53, contains several prophecies which Jesus fulfilled, and further to that, several of them tie with prophecies given by another prophet, Daniel, and they also tie back to certain Verses that are in Chapter 1, of the Book of Isaiah.

First I want to address the prophecy in Isaiah 53, Verse 3, which states, "He is despised and rejected of men; and we esteemed him not." Jesus' fulfilled that prophecy through these sections of Verses 29, 30 and 32 in Lection 81, which tell us, "Pilate said, I have found no cause of death in him: I will therefore chastise him, and let him go. *And they were instant with loud voices, requiring that he might be crucified.* And the voices of them and of the chief priests prevailed. And Pilate gave sentence that it should be as they required. And he delivered Iesus to their will."

It's important to note: they who despised and rejected Jesus were solely those of the Israelites, for only they demanded He be put to death. The Romans did not want to put Jesus to death, as Pilate could find no fault with him; however, the chief Hebrew priests insisted He be crucified. Why? It had been for many reasons, but the actual reason the chief priests seized upon, had been due to the fact Jesus had violated Moses' Passover Law, when He refused to allow the Passover lamb Judas had bought, to be slaughtered.

Jesus fulfilled the next prophecies, which are in Verses 5, 6, 8, 10 and 11, through different sections of Verse 32 within Lection 81, and when looking at Isaiah, 53, Verse 5, we find three prophecies in the Verse: But he was wounded for our transgressions; and he was bruised for our iniquities; and the chastisement of our peace was upon him; and with his stripes we are healed. Those prophecies were fulfilled by this section of Lection 81, Verse 32, "And Pilate gave sentence that it should be as they required. And he delivered Jesus to their will."

Isaiah 53, Verse 6, not only contains a prophecy which Jesus fulfilled, it also contains important, revealing information. First I'll address the prophecy, which is this section of Verse 6, "the LORD hath laid on him the iniquity of us all," and this section of Verse 32, in Lection 81, fulfills that prophecy, "Then answered all the people, and said, His blood be on us and on our children."

What was the iniquity that had been laid on Jesus, and whose iniquity had it been? Isaiah, Chapter 1 tells us whose iniquity it had been, by this statement in Verse 4, "Ah sinful nation, *a people laden with iniquity*, a seed of evildoers, children that are corrupters: they have forsaken the LORD." Who is the sinful nation laden with iniquity? It is the Israelites only, for no other nation is identified. Why are the Israelites sinful?

That answer is found in Verses 11 through 16 in Isaiah, Chapter 1:

11 *To what purpose is the multitude of your sacrifices unto me?* saith the LORD: *I am full of the burnt offerings of rams, and the fat of fed beasts; and I delight not in the blood of bullocks, or of lambs, or of he goats.*
12 *When ye come to appear before me, who hath required this at your hand,* to tread my courts?
13 *Bring no more vain oblations*; incense is an abomination unto me; the new moons and sabbaths, the calling of assemblies, I cannot away with; *it is iniquity*, even the solemn meeting.
14 *Your new moons and your appointed feasts my soul hateth*: they are a trouble unto me; I am weary to bear them.

44

15 And when ye spread forth your hands, I will hide mine eyes from you: yea, when ye make many prayers, I will not hear: *your hands are full of blood.*

16 Wash you, make you clean; *put away the evil of your doings from before mine eyes*; cease to do evil;

Wow! Those six Verses certainly make it clear the blood sacrifices, carried out in accordance with the blood sacrifice laws for the atonement of sin within Exodus 29, were not of the Lord. That is made clear in Verse 12, when the Lord tells Isaiah, *"When ye come to appear before me, who hath required this at your hand?"*

Then in Verses 14, 15 and 16, the Lord crystallizes the fact that He hates the blood sacrifices, and deems them to be evil. What is evil? Evil is any morally wrong act in principle or practice, and something that is morally wrong in principle or practice is sin, or to put it another way: it is iniquity. It is clear the blood sacrifices that the Lord hates, are transgressions against His Laws, and obviously His Laws contradict the blood sacrifice rituals and laws in Exodus 29.

I also mentioned that Isaiah 53:6 has important and revealing information, which is, "All we like sheep have gone astray; we have turned every one to his own way." Why is it important? It ties directly with Verse 6 within Chapter 50 of the Book of Jeremiah, which states, "My people hath been lost sheep: their shepherds have caused them to go astray, they have turned them away on the mountains: they have gone from mountain to hill, they have forgotten their restingplace."

Who are the shepherds who caused them to go astray? They are those, who after Moses' death, wrote the Laws the Lord had given to Moses, but when they did, as Apostle Peter made clear in The Clementine Homilies, they added falsehoods, and obviously one had been the blood sacrifice rituals and laws for the atonement of sin in Exodus 29. The

45

Israelites, the sheep, by obeying those false laws, went astray. By the way, not only does Isaiah, Chapter 1, make it clear that only the Israelites were being addressed, so does Verse 6 of Jeremiah, Chapter 50, for once again, no other nation had been named.

The next prophecy of Isaiah 53, is this section in Verse 8, "He was taken from prison and from judgment," and this section of Verse 32, within Lection 81 fulfilled it, "Pilate gave sentence that it should be as they required. And he delivered Jesus to their will."

Verse 8 of Isaiah 53, also tells us, "for he was cut off out of the land of the living," and "for the transgression of my people was he stricken." These are significant prophecies, for they were also given by the prophet Daniel. First I'll address "the transgression" which is spoken to in Verses 11 and 12 within Chapter 8 of the Book of Daniel. Those Verses tell us the prince of the host took away the daily [blood] sacrifice by reason of transgression. Verse 25 of Chapter 9 tells us the prince of the host is the Messiah, and Verse 23 of Chapter 8 tells us when the transgressors are come to the full.

What was the transgression the Messiah had been stricken for? According to the prophet Daniel, it was for the daily blood sacrifice carried out in the temple, for the atonement of sin, as directed through the blood sacrifice rituals and laws of Exodus, Chapter 29. And who were the transgressors the Messiah had been stricken for? They were the Israelites, for only the sins, iniquities and transgressions of the Israelites were identified, no other nation was mentioned.

Next we have this section Isaiah 53, Verse 8: "for he was cut off out of the land of the living," and that ties directly with this section of Daniel, Chapter 9, Verse 24, "to finish the transgression, and to make an end of sins, and to make reconciliation for iniquity," which ties with this part of

46

Verse 26, "shall Messiah be cut off, but not for himself," and that ties directly with this section of Verse 27, "and in the midst of the week he shall cause the sacrifice and the oblation to cease." The Messiah finished the transgression and made an end of sins and made reconciliation for iniquity when He was cut off for the Israelites, in the midst of the week, which is when He suffered His crucifixion.

The prophecies Jesus fulfilled in Isaiah 53:10-11, are these sections of the Verses: Verse 10, "when thou shalt make his soul an offering for sin;" and in Verse 11, "for he shall bear their iniquities." And these prophecies too, were fulfilled by this section of Verse 32 in Lection 81, "Then answered all the people, and said, His blood be on us and on our children."

Next, Jesus fulfilled the prophecy in this section of Verse 7 within Isaiah 53: "He was oppressed, and he was afflicted, yet he opened not his mouth." Lection 81, Verse 16, fulfilled that prophecy thru this part of the Verse, "Then he questioned with him in many words, but he answered him nothing."

The last of the prophecies within today's reading of Isaiah 53, are these sections of Verse 12: "he was numbered with the transgressors; and he bare the sin of many, and made intercession for the transgressors." This section of Verse 9 in Lection 82, "And there were also two other malefactors led with him to be put to death," fulfills this section of Isaiah 53:12, "he was numbered with the transgressors," and these sections of Isaiah 53:12, "he bare the sin of many, and made intercession for the transgressors," were fulfilled by this section of Lection 10, Verse 3, "by righteousness taketh away the sin of the world."

Whose sin did Jesus bear, and who were the transgressors that He made intercession for? They were for the sins and transgressions of the Israelites only, for no other nation had been identified.

47

The first sentence in Verse 3 of Lection 10, "THE next day John [the Baptist] saw Jesus coming unto him, and said, Behold the Lamb of God, which by righteousness taketh away the sin of the world," warrants further discussion. That section is also found in John 1, Verse 29 which reads, "The next day John seeth Jesus coming unto him, and saith, Behold the Lamb of God, which taketh away the sin of the world."

Why is further discussion important? It is due to the fact that most Christians quote that standalone Verse as proof Jesus died on the cross to redeem mankind of their sins, and they do that with confidence for there are no other lessons in the New Testament to alter that concept. However, Jesus' Gospel recorded by Apostle John, provides full disclosure, and leaves nothing to one's imagination, which often is the case within the New Testament.

What do I mean by that statement? There are lessons in the New Testament which bring the savvy reader, the discerning reader, to a point wherein they cannot arrive at a defined conclusion. Sure, they can interpolate to arrive at a conclusion, but in reality, interpolation is nothing more than a guess.

I'll explain the difference between full disclosure, and scripture which leaves one in limbo. John the Baptist had already made it very clear in Verse 10 of Lection 7, that the blood sacrifice will not eliminate sin, when he said, "Keep yourselves from blood and things strangled and from dead bodies of birds and beasts, and from all deeds of cruelty, and from all that is gotten of wrong; Think ye the blood of beasts and birds will wash away sin! I tell you Nay, Speak the Truth. Be just, Be merciful to one another and to all creatures that live, and walk humbly with your God."

That very important information preached by John the Baptist had been eliminated from New Testament scripture,

48

and in doing such, when one reads John 1:29, "The next day John seeth Jesus coming unto him, and saith, Behold the Lamb of God, which taketh away the sin of the world," they can come to only one conclusion: Jesus, when He died on the cross, redeemed mankind of their sin.

In further support to that which John the Baptist stated in Lection 7:10, "Think ye the blood of beasts and birds will wash away sin! I tell you Nay," in Lection 33, Verse 2, Jesus crystallized the fact that the blood sacrifice does not remit sin, when He stated, "No blood offering, of beast or bird, or man, can take away sin, for how can the conscience be purged from sin by the shedding of innocent blood? Nay, it will increase the condemnation."

Please note that Jesus added "man," and that fact in-and-of-itself negates Pharisee Saul/Paul's statements in Romans 8:3, wherein he claimed God sent His Son in the likeness of sinful flesh, and for sin, condemned sin in the flesh, and in Romans 10:9-10, wherein he stated those who believe in Jesus and confess, shall be saved.

Wow! No wonder so many Christians do not want to even look at any information that could set aside that belief – for they are convinced, due to Pharisee Saul/Paul's false teachings in Jesus' Name, they have been saved! But steadfastly believing in Pharisee Saul/Paul's false teachings, and refusing to even look at any biblical writings which contradict that belief, does nothing except fill the trap that has been set by children of the wicked one.

Verse 9 of today's reading of Jesus' Gospel, told us, "Verily I say unto you, for this end have I come into the world, that I may put away all blood offerings and the eating of the flesh of the beasts and the birds that are slain by men," and in Verse 11 He told His chosen Twelve, "Not by shedding innocent blood, therefore, but by living a righteous life, shall ye find the peace of God."

The statements He made in those Verses certainly dot the I's and cross the T's regarding the Verses I shared with you pursuant to the blood sacrifice, as the Lord addressed it in Isaiah, Chapter 1, and as the blood sacrifice is covered in the Verses within Chapters 8 and 9 of the Book of Daniel. Combined, all those Verses provide crucially important information that has been twisted to convey a message that had not been intended. Why is that so?

Most Christians, who firmly believe they have been saved, do so because they hang their hat on the false teachings of Pharisee Saul/Paul: that Christ had died on the cross to redeem mankind from their sins, and many support their belief by quoting the prophecies Jesus fulfilled in Isaiah, Chapter 53, for they believe those prophecies apply to all people. However, you now know the basis for their belief has been built on a false foundation, for the Isaiah 53 prophecies Jesus fulfilled, addressed only the Israelites, and no other nation.

Brothers and Sisters, what a wonderful gift it is that we can give to those souls who think Jesus died on the cross to save them, by giving them the true knowledge Jesus brought into the world; they will then know they must steadfastly walk the steps to salvation, which His Father had given, and He reestablished.

Once given this knowledge, those you help will have an opportunity to achieve the purity required to gain entry into the Kingdom of Heaven. I encourage you with my whole heart, soul and mind to take up Jesus' Cross, as I and others have done, and share with as many people as possible, God's and His Son's Truths that have been hidden through the efforts of the children of the wicked one.

Chapter 9

Homily: A discussion of 2 Samuel 24 lessons as they apply to Jesus' Doctrine recorded by Apostle John.

Brothers and Sisters, I have a few comments that I want to make regarding today's reading of the Old Testament, 2 Samuel, Chapter 24, Verses 12 through 25. But before beginning my comments, I want to bring to your attention a new, but old law Jesus gave to His chosen Twelve, which is within His Gospel recorded by Apostle John.

This law given by Jesus during the Last Paschal Supper, is in Lection 76, Verse 5, which states, "A new commandment I give unto you, that ye love one another and all the creatures of God. Love is the fulfilling of the law. Love is of God, and God is love. Whoso loveth not, knoweth not God."

In addition, I want to bring to your attention a few lessons Jesus gave regarding the forgiveness of sin, with the first being in Lection 93, Verse 1. "Iesus said, God forgiveth all sin to those who repent, but as ye sow, so also must ye reap. If one being in the spirit seeth clearly that any repent and forsake their sins, such may truly say unto the penitent, Thy sins are forgiven thee, for All sin is remitted by repentance and amendment and they are loosed from it, who forsake it and bound to it, who continue it."

And, in Verse 2, Jesus said, "Nevertheless the fruits of the sin must continue for a season, for as we sow so must we reap, for God is not mocked," and in Lection 69 Verse 3, Jesus stated, "For them that have done evil there is no rest, but they go out and in, and suffer correction for ages, till they are made perfect. But for them that have done good and attained unto perfection, there is endless rest and they go into life everlasting. They rest in the Eternal."

Then in Verse 11 of Lection 67, Jesus addressed evil souls, when He stated, "Then shall he say also unto them on his left hand, Depart from me ye evil souls into the eternal fires which ye have prepared for yourselves, till ye are purified seven times and cleansed from your sins," and in Verse 15, He said, "And the cruel and the loveless shall go away into chastisement for ages, and if they repent not, be utterly destroyed."

The Verses I just shared, crystallize the fact God is love, and they clarify He will forgive sin, as long as a soul repents and amends its behavior. However, Jesus made a point that is important to take note of: even though a sin is forgiven, the soul still has penance to pay, for God is not mocked. In addition, those Verses also paint a clear picture that God has a plan in place, and that plan will govern the suffering a soul must endure for sins committed, and it also will prescribe the suffering a soul will bear in Hades, for evil acts it had perpetrated upon other souls.

Now I'll apply the information I've shared with you to the scripture that tells us about the two malefactors who were crucified along with Jesus, but I must point out that scripture does not tell us anything more about them, other than the fact they were admitted malefactors. On the other hand, scripture does tell us, Barabbas, whom the Jews demanded to be set free, rather than Jesus, had been a robber and a murderer. Being there is no information to the contrary, I could assume both malefactors being crucified along with Jesus, were also robbers and murderers, but being I do not know for sure, I'll err on the side of being nonjudgmental, and assume they were robbers, and not murderers.

With that being stated, one of the malefactors said to Jesus in Verse 16 of Lection 82, "Lord remember me when thou comest into thy kingdom." "And Iesus said unto him, Verily I say unto thee, to day shalt thou be with me in Paradise."

Paradise is a very important place I must further address. In Lection 37, Verses 1 and 2, as Jesus sat in the porch of the Temple, He told His disciples, "Blessed are they who suffer many experiences, for they shall be made perfect through suffering: they shall be as the angels of God in Heaven and shall die no more, neither shall they be born any more, for death and birth have no more dominion over them."

And then He said in Verse 7, "When it [a soul] cometh from the darkness, it is that he hath lived before, and when it goeth down again into darkness, it is that he may rest for a little, and thereafter again exist."

Keeping in mind Jesus' statement to the malefactor, "Verily I say unto thee, to day shalt thou be with me in Paradise," I want you to think about this for a moment: in Lection 37, Verse 7, Jesus stated, "when it [a soul] goeth down again into darkness, it is that he may rest for a little, and thereafter again exist."

It is very important that you understand this fact: there is a difference between Paradise and Heaven, and Verses 8 and 9 of Lection 65, shed light on that fact. In Verse 8 Jesus stated, "Put ye not off from day to day, and from cycle to cycle and eon to eon, in the belief, that when ye return to this world ye will succeed in gaining the mysteries, and entering into the Kingdom of Light," and then He said in Verse 9, "For ye know not when the number of perfected souls shall be filled up, and then will be shut the gates of the Kingdom of Light, and from hence none will be able to come in thereby, nor will any go forth."

Those Verses elucidate the fact that the Kingdom of Light – the Kingdom of Heaven, is not Paradise, but a completely different place, which looks down upon Paradise. Where does a soul rest? It rests in Paradise. Being Paradise is where Jesus told the malefactor he would be that very day, could it be that the malefactor would proceed on to the eternal fires in Hades to be purified? It is possible, based upon the lessons Jesus taught in the Verses I have shared with you, especially if the malefactor had committed that which is referred to as mortal sin.

Based upon the lessons Jesus taught, it is my humble opinion that those souls who have committed only venial sin, are the souls who rest in Paradise, before experiencing another life in its effort to achieve the purification required to enter into the Kingdom of Light.

All of the information I've thus far shared, sheds light on the fact that there are three places to which a soul goes when it passes back over to the invisible, from whence it came: Paradise, Heaven and Hades. Keep in mind that Jesus taught there is no eternal damnation in hell, as many religions teach; for he taught that a soul, who refuses to amend its ways to those of God, will eventually be utterly destroyed.

What is the point of all the lessons within the Gospel of the Holy Twelve that I have just shared with you, as they relate to 2 Samuel 24:12-25? The point is that these lessons contradict lessons in 2 Samuel 24. For example, in Verses 12 through 16, of today's reading of 2 Samuel 24, we were told Gad was to go to David, so he may choose one of three punishments for sinning. Think about this: why would that be when God has just punishments that will be implemented, based upon sins committed, when a soul returns to the invisible?

In Verse 14, David chose three days of pestilence in the land, and then in verse 15, we are told that resulted in the death of 70,000 men. That's a very serious punishment, set upon 70,000 men, who in all reality could have been innocent bystanders, who had absolutely nothing to do with the sins of David. That retribution reminds me of the story regarding the Lord hardening Pharaoh's heart in Exodus, so he would not allow the Israelites to leave Egypt, and then

54

told Moses: when Pharaoh did such, He would kill the firstborn of Pharaoh that sitteth upon his throne, even unto the firstborn of the maidservant that is behind the mill; and all the firstborn of beasts.

Based upon the Verses I shared with you from Jesus' Gospel, which made clear God is very forgiving, and that God is of love - do those stories within 2 Samuel, and Exodus, make any sense? To help in determining that answer, let's examine Verses 18 through 25, within 2 Samuel 24, wherein we are told that Gad told David to build unto the Lord an altar, and then give an oxen as burnt offerings.

When determining an answer, one must weigh heavily this fact: the message conveyed in Verses 18 through 25, certainly ties with the blood covenant of Exodus 24, and the blood sacrifice rituals and laws of Exodus 29, and those of you who have previously participated in our worship services, know that the blood covenant, and sacrifice rituals and laws for the atonement of sin, are not of God, but of men to suit their needs and traditions. And being those Verses are not of God, that reality gives credence to this fact: the Verses wherein God visited 3 days of pestilence upon David, and 70,000 men were killed, must also be of men.

Brothers and Sisters in Christ, I humbly call upon you to be a warrior for God and His Son, and I ask you to put on the full armor of God through your faith in Him, and I urge you to please share with many people as you can, the truths I share with you, and I ask you to confirm in your heart the importance of doing such, by reading the dreams and visions of Anointed Prophets, Russell and Paul Maddock, which they have shared on RodCDavis.com.

When you log on, scroll down to the Worship Service & Updates button, and after clicking on it, click on the "Go To Now" button that is within: God & the Holy Spirit -

Prophetic Dreams & Visions picture. Once you have read that which the Maddock brothers have revealed, I firmly believe you will be inspired to share that link with as many people as you possibly can.

Chapter 10

Gospel Reading: Ezekiel 2 & 4 - Reading from Jesus'
Gospel: Lesson 68 & 76

Homily: By Anointed Prophets, Paul & Russell Maddock, as guided by the Holy Spirit

Brothers and Sisters, while preparing this worship service, this thought interrupted my concentration as I structured the homily: ask Anointed Prophets Russell and Paul Maddock to choose the 28th Sabbath / Sunday worship service reading of the Old Testament, along with the reading from the Gospel of the Holy Twelve, and in addition, ask them to prepare the Homily.

Being that thought interrupted my concentration, I knew the thought had not been mine, and I knew it came from Holy Spirit. I asked Anointed Prophets Russell and Paul if they would be willing to do such, and when I did, I learned that Paul had recently been given information that fit right into that which I had asked of them.

A few days after I received that which I had requested from the Maddock Brothers, spiritual guidance told me I must present the reading of the Old Testament, and of the Gospel of the Holy Twelve, and the homily, in the manner in which they had delivered it to me. Thus being, the reading of the Old Testament, and the reading of the Gospel of the Holy Twelve, and the Homily, have all been melded into one. From this point on, that which I share will be as though the Maddock Brothers, themselves, were speaking the words.

In the Old Testament, God speaks through His anointed prophet Ezekiel, to confront the rebellious house of Israel, who has transgressed the Law He gave.

Ezekiel 2:1-5.

1. And he said unto me, Son of man, stand upon thy feet, and I will speak unto thee.

2. And the Spirit entered into me when he spake unto me, and set me upon my feet, that I heard him that spake unto me.

3. And he said unto me, Son of man, I send thee to the children of Israel, to a rebellious nation that hath rebelled against me: they and their fathers have transgressed against me, even unto this very day.

4. For they are impudent children and stiffhearted. I do send thee unto them; and thou shalt say unto them, Thus saith the Lord God.

5. And they, whether they will hear, or whether they will forbear, (for they are a rebellious house,) yet shall they know that there hath been a prophet among them.

Ezekiel 2:8-10.

8. But thou, son of man, hear what I say unto thee; Be not thou rebellious like that rebellious house: open thou mouth, and eat that I give thee.

9. And when I looked, behold, an hand was sent unto me; and, lo, a roll of a book was therein;

10. And he spread it before me; and it was written within and without: and there was written therein lamentations, and mourning, and woe.

In Verses 8 through 10, God told Ezekiel he would be a sign unto the rebellious house of Israel, to make known to them, their devilment in His sight. And, if they rejected the correction God sent through Ezekiel, as punishment, they would be sent into captivity.

Ezekiel 4:9-17.

9. Take thou also unto thee wheat, and barley, and beans, and lentils, and millet, and fitches, and put them in one vessel, and make thee bread thereof, according to the number of the days that thou shalt lie upon thy side, three hundred and ninety days shalt thou eat thereof.

10. And thy meat which thou shalt eat shall be by weight, twenty shekels a day: from time to time shalt thou eat it.

11. Thou shalt drink also water by measure, the sixth part of an hin: from time to time shalt thou drink.

12. And thou shalt eat it as barley cakes, and thou shalt bake it with dung that cometh out of man in their sight.

13. And the LORD said, Even thus shall the children eat their defiled bread among the Gentiles, whither I will drive them.

14. Then said I, Ah Lord GOD! behold, my soul hath not been polluted: for my youth up even till now have I not eaten of that which dieth of itself, or is torn in pieces; neither came there abominable flesh into my mouth.

15. Then he said unto me, Lo, I have given cow's dung for man's dung, and thou shalt prepare thy bread therewith.

16. Moreover he said unto me, Son of man, behold, I will break the staff of bread in Jerusalem: and they shall eat

bread by weight, and with care; and they shall drink water by measure, and with astonishment:

17. That they may want bread and water, and be astonied one with another, and consume away for their iniquity.

From the Gospel of the Holy Twelve

The Householder And The Husbandmen Order Out Of Disorder,

Lection LXVIII Verses 1-14.

1. AND Jesus said, Hear another parable: There was a certain householder, who planted a vineyard, and hedged it round about and digged a winepress in it, and built a tower, and let it out to husbandmen and went into a fare country.

2. And when the time of the ripe fruits drew near, he sent his servants to the husbandmen that they might receive the fruits of it. And the husbandmen took his servants and beat one, and stoned another, and killed another.

3. Again he sent other servants, more honourable than the first, and they did unto them likewise. But last of all he sent unto them his son, saying, They will reverence my son.

4. But when the husbandmen saw the son, they said among themselves. This is the heir, come let us kill him, and let us seize on his inheritance. and they caught him and cast him out of the vineyard and slew him.

5. When the lord of the vineyard cometh what will he do unto those husbandmen? They say unto him, He will miserable destroy those wicked men and let out his vineyard to other husbandmen, which shall render him the fruits in their seasons.

6. Jesus saith unto them, Did ye never read in the scriptures, The Stone which the builders rejected, the same has become the head of the Pyramid? this is the Lord's doing and it is marvelous in our eyes?

7. Therefore I say unto you, The kingdom of God shall be taken from you and given to a nation bringing forth the fruits thereof. And whosoever shall fall on this Stone shall be broken, but on whomsoever it shall fall, it will grind them to powder.

8. And when the chief priests and the Pharisees had heard his parables, they perceived that he spake of them. But when they sought to lay hands on him they feared the multitude, because they took him for a prophet.

9. And the disciples ask him afterwards the meaning of this parable, and he said unto them, The vineyard is the world, the husbandmen are your priests, and the messengers are the servants of the good Law, and the Prophets.

10. When the fruits of their labour are demanded of the priests, none are given, but they evilly treat the messengers who teach the truth of God, even as they have done from the beginning.

11. And when the Son of Man cometh. even the Christ of God, they gather together against the Holy One, and slay him, and cast him out of the vineyard, for they have not wrought the things of the Spirit, but sought their own pleasure and gain rejecting the holy Law.

12. Had they accepted the Anointed One, who is the corner stone and the head, it would have been well with them, and the Building would have stood, even as the Temple of God inhabited by the Spirit.

13. But the day will come when the Law which they reject shall become the head stone, seen of all, and they who stumble on it shall be broken, but they who persist in disobedience shall be ground to pieces.

14. For to some of the angles God gave dominion over the course of this world, charging them to rule in wisdom, in justice and in love. But they have neglected the commands of the Most High, and rebelled against the good order of God. Thus cruelty and suffering and sorrow hath entered the world, till the time the Master returns, and taketh possession of all things, and calleth his servants to account.

Verses 1 through 14 that I just read, which are within Lection LXVIII of the Gospel of the Holy Twelve, portray the age old fight against the True teachings of Almighty God. Verses 9 and 10 declared the husbandmen, identified as being priests in the parable, had defiled the Lord's true teachings, and evilly treated the messengers and prophets God sent, which He had done to reassert His good Law. When the fruits of the labor of the messengers and prophets were demanded from the priests, none was given, for the priests had not obeyed, and instead fulfilled their own desires, and thus being, they evilly treated the messengers who taught the truth of God, even as had been done from the beginning.

Christ, in Verses 11 through 14, proclaims the teachings of the good Law would bring order out of their disorder, but the priests would not accept it. Now, in this age, which is soon to be the end of the Church age, Almighty God is going to send His Two Witnesses, to once again, bring order to the defiled Churches, which are out of order according to the Law of Love.

It's important to note that Jesus taught in Lection 46, Verse 24, "This is the new Law unto the Israel of God, and the Law is within, for it is the Law of Love, and it is not new but old. Take heed that ye add nothing to this law, neither take anything from it. Verily I say unto you, they who believe and obey this law shall be saved, and they who know and obey it not, shall be lost."

Jesus certainly made it very clear, the Law of Love is to be embraced from the heart, and followed to the *Letter, and if you do not, watch out!*

The Transfiguration on the Mount The Giving Of the Law

Lection XLVI, Verses 7 through 21

7. AND Jesus said unto them, Behold a new law I give unto you, which is not new but old. Even as Moses gave the Ten Commandments to Israel after the flesh, so also I give unto you the Twelve for the Kingdom of Israel after the Spirit.

8. For who are the Israel of God? Even they of every nation and tribe who work righteousness, love mercy and keep my commandments, these are the true Israel of God. And standing upon his feet, Jesus spake, saying:

9. Hear O Israel, JOVA, they God is One; many are My seers, and My prophets. In Me all live and move, and have subsistence.

10. Ye shall not take away the life of any creature for your pleasure, nor for your profit nor yet torment it.

11. Ye shall not steal the goods of any, nor gather lands and riches to yourselves, beyond your need or use.

63

12. Ye shall not eat the flesh, nor drink the blood of any slaughtered creature, nor yet anything which bringeth disorder to your health or senses.

13. Ye shall not make impure marriages, where love and health are not, nor yet corrupt yourselves, or any creature made pure by the Holy.

14. Ye shall not bear false witness against any, nor willfully deceive any by a lie to hurt them.

15. Ye shall not do unto others, as ye would not that others should do unto you.

16. Ye shall worship One Eternal, the Father-Mother in Heaven, of Whom are all things, and reverence the Holy Name.

17. Ye shall revere your fathers and your mothers on earth, whose care is for you, and all the Teachers of Righteousness.

18. Ye shall cherish and protect the week, and those who are oppressed, and all creatures who suffer wrong.

19. Ye shall work with your hands the things that are good and seemly; so shall ye eat the fruits of the earth, and live long in the land.

20. Ye shall purify yourselves daily and rest the Seventh day from labour, keeping holy the Sabbaths and the Festival of your God.

21. Ye shall do unto others as ye would that others should do unto you.

Paul and myself, as God's Two Witnesses, along with Reverend Roderick C. Davis, have been called and anointed to bring together the Body of Christ, in which a *mighty army of called and faithful believers,* will be assembled and made ready to go to battle.

Jesus Foretelleth The End

Lection LXI 3-6.

3. And in those days those that have power shall gather to themselves the lands and riches of the earth for their own lusts, and shall oppress the many who lack and hold them in bondage, and use them to increase their riches, and they shall oppress even the beasts of the field, setting up the abominable thing. But God shall send them his messenger and they shall proclaim his laws, which men have hidden by their traditions, and those that transgress shall die.

4. Then shall they deliver you up to be afflicted, and shall kill you; and ye shall be hated of all nations for my Name's sake. And then shall many be offended, and shall betray one another, and shall hate one another. And many false prophets shall rise, and shall deceive many.

5. And because iniquity shall abound, the love of many shall wax cold. But he that shall endure unto the end, the same shall be saved. *And this gospel of the kingdom shall be preached in all the world for a witness unto all nations; and then shall the end come.*

The Verses we just shared, made this very clear: if correction is not received by the people, and embraced whole heartedly, great judgment is soon to come. In the same likeness, when the prophets of God were sent in times past to correct that which had been changed by men, Almighty God will deal with those who vehemently stand in opposition to His spoken words, which at this time, come through my brother Paul, and myself.

In Lection LXXVI of the Gospel of the Holy Twelve, **The Washing Of Feet The Eucharistic Oblation,** Verses 5 and 6, Jesus crystallized the fact that love is the fulfilling of the Law:

5. A new commandment I give unto you, that ye love one another and all the creatures of God. *Love is the fulfilling of the Law.* Love is of God, and God is love. Who so loveth not, noweth not God.

6. Now ye are clean through the word which I have spoken unto you. By this shall all men know that ye are my disciples if ye have love one to another and show mercy and love to all creatures of God, especially to those that are week and oppressed and suffer wrong. For the whole earth is filled with dark places of cruelty, and with pain and sorrow, by the selfishness and ignorance of man.

Jesus made it very clear in Verses 5 and 6, love is to be shown not only to one another, but also to *all creatures of God*, and that factor is one of the significant dividing lines between the true teachings of Christ, and those who follow the counterfeit teachings within the New Testament, that are of Pharisee Saul/Paul.

What exactly are the major factors that create the division? One is the eating of flesh, and the other is the lessons Pharisee Saul/Paul preached, wherein he represented Jesus' crucifixion had been a blood sacrifice to redeem all of mankind from their sins. Why did Pharisee Saul/Paul preach such? As a Pharisee, Saul had been an advocate and protector of the blood covenant of Exodus 24, and the blood sacrifice rituals and laws for the atonement of sin in

Exodus 29, and he did not change after becoming Paul. That counterfeit doctrine Saul/Paul preached, is part and parcel to the defiled Church, which is known as the **Great Whore of Babylon.**

In Revelation, Chapter 17, John was shown the Great Whore of Babylon, which is the Mother of Harlots, and the Abominations of the Earth, who was drunken with the blood of the saints, and with the blood of the martyrs of Jesus.

In Revelation, Chapter 18, Verses 1 through 24, we are told about the judgment of the Great Whore, who is symbolic of the Roman Catholic Church, and her offspring, the Protestant Churches, both of which exalt and teach Pauline doctrine, in which it is proclaimed Christ had been a blood sacrifice to redeem mankind from their sin, and being they represent it to be the genuine teachings of Christ, *they will be judged!*

During this time, Almighty God will be speaking through His two anointed servants, and the genuine Body of Christ. The hatred toward the words His anointed prophets will speak, will be enormous, and their distinct message, delivered through the love of God, will be unmistakable.

Revelation, Chapter 18, Verses 4 through 8

4. And I heard another voice from heaven, saying, *Come out of her, my people, that ye be not partakers of her sins, and that ye receive not of her plagues.*

5. For her sins have reached unto heaven, and God hath remembered her iniquities.

6. Reward her even as she rewarded you, and double unto her double according to her works: in the cup which she hath filled fill to her double.

7. How much she hath glorified herself, and lived deliciously, so much torment and sorrow give her: For she saith in her heart, I sit a queen, and am no widow, and shall see no sorrow.

8. Therefore shall her plagues come in one day, death, and mourning, and famine; and she shall be utterly burned with fire: for strong is the Lord God who judges her.

In preparation for that which is to come to pass in our generation, God has guided us to Reverend Roderick C. Davis, who is called and anointed to teach the genuine teachings of Jesus Christ, our Lord and King. In the times ahead, the Spirit of Almighty God, is going to gather together a Mighty Army of called and faithful followers who will be prepared to do battle against the falsehoods of the Great Whore.

The battle will be a hard fought one. There is no doubt, there will be casualties. Our heart felt hope and prayer will be that many will harken to God's call implemented thru His prophets and faithful servants, and denounce the false teachings of Pauline Christianity, wherein sits Satan's throne, and become part of the genuine Body of Christ.

Paul and myself were given many dreams and visions, before the Spirit of Almighty God directed us to the Gospel of the Holy Twelve. The Holy Spirit spoke unto us: when you read scriptures that line up with your dreams and visions, know that you are on the correct path. To say the least, we were overwhelmed with great joy when we read the genuine teachings of our Lord Jesus Christ, within the Gospel of the Holy Twelve.

Now we have scripture to back up our dreams and visions. We are both very thankful to Reverend Roderick C. Davis, and his kind heart toward us, to give us this opportunity to proclaim that which had been given to us by the Holy Spirit. Truly the Lord God is fighting for the lost children of Israel, to bring then out of spiritual bondage. It is very exciting to see the Body of Christ working together in Spirit and in Truth.

In closing, I would like to refer to the 4th Chapter of Isaiah, to drive home the point of all the information which my brother and I have shared: ***Only by keeping ALL the Law of Love in it's fullness, and by doing so with genuine heart felt Love, will one be considered a son or daughter of the Most High God.***

Isaiah 4:1-6

1. And in that day seven women shall take hold of one man, saying, ***We will eat our own bread, and wear our own apparel: only let us be called by thy name, to take away our reproach.***

2. In that day shall the branch of the Lord be beautiful and glorious, and the fruit of the earth shall be excellent and comely ***for them that are escaped of Israel.***

3. And it shall come to pass, ***that he that is left in Zion, and he that remaineth in Jerusalem, shall be called holy, even everyone that is written among the living in Jerusalem:***

4. When the Lord shall have ***washed away the filth of the daughters of Zion, and shall have purged the blood of***

69

Jerusalem from the midst thereof by the spirit of judgment, and by the spirit of burning.

5. And the Lord will create upon every dwelling place of mount Zion, and upon her assemblies, a cloud and smoke by day, and the shinning of a flaming fire by night: for upon all the glory shall be a defence.

6. And there shall be a tabernacle for a shadow in the day time from the heat, and for a place of refuge, and for a covert from the storm and from rain.

May all praise, glory and honor be unto Almighty God, Christ Jesus and Holy Spirit.

Humble servants of Christ Jesus, Paul and Russell Maddock

Chapter 11

Homily Discussion of Deuteronomy Lessons, Chapters 1-12, as they apply to lessons in Jesus' Gospel recorded by Apostle John.

Brothers and Sisters, before discussing Verses in Deuteronomy, Chapter 12, I want to bring to your attention certain lessons taught in Chapters 1 through 11. Moses addressed often the fact that he journeyed up a mountain in Horeb, and stood between the Lord and his followers, while learning from the Lord that which He wanted to command the Israelites to do. In addition to the Commandments that were given, the Israelites were told that the Lord wanted them to leave Horeb, and journey to certain other lands to possess them.

The Lord told the Israelites not to fear or be discouraged, for He will go before them, and fight for them as he did in Egypt. However, the Lord did tell Moses, that while on their way to the certain lands He wanted them to possess, they would pass certain groups of people on other lands, and He said they must not meddle with them. Further, there is an accounting by the Lord, of His destruction of people who had possessed the land, prior to those who now possess it.

Then in Verse 24 of Deuteronomy 2, the Lord said, "Rise ye up, take your journey, and pass over the river Arnon: behold, I have given into thine hand Sihon the Amorite, king of Heshbon, and his land: begin to possess it, and contend with him in battle." And then in Verse 30 we are told, "But Sihon king of Heshbon would not let us pass by him: for the LORD thy God hardened his spirit, and made his heart obstinate, that he might deliver him into thy hand, as appeareth this day."

Verse 30 is certainly reminiscent of the story told in Exodus, wherein the Lord hardened Pharaoh's heart, so he

71

would not allow the Jews to leave Egypt, and that is just one aspect within Deuteronomy, Chapters 1 through 11, that is similar to stories within Exodus.

Then, in Deuteronomy, Chapter 2, Verses 31 through 36, a story is conveyed wherein the Lord delivered Sihon to the Israelites, and they took all of his cities, and utterly destroyed the men, and the women, and the children, and left none to remain. Next they went to do battle with the king of Bashan, and did to all of those within his kingdom, as they did to those within the Kingdom of Sihon. Wow! That is certainly contradictory to God's Law of Love given by Jesus. Would the Lord our God, truly have instructed the Israelites to do such?

Then in Deuteronomy, Chapter 4, the Lord told Moses to hearken unto the statutes and judgments he is going to teach, and said, "*Ye shall not add unto the word which I command you, neither shall ye diminish ought from it, that ye may keep the commandments of the LORD your God which I command you.*" Moses taught those statutes and judgments, as the Lord had commanded, which were the 10 Commandments, and three of them were:

6 – thou shall not kill;
8 - thou shall not steal; and
10 – thou shall not covet anything that belongs to your neighbor.

Please keep those commandments in mind, as I will be referring to them again.

In Deuteronomy, Chapter 6, it is written that the Israelites are to obey those commandments in the land they now possess, and included in that land, were houses full of good things that they did not earn, and wells they did not dig, and vineyards and olive trees that they did not plant, all of which came into their hands as a result of their destruction

72

of the people who had been occupying the land, and all that it contained.

In Deuteronomy, Chapter 7, it is written in Verse 6, "For thou art an holy people unto the LORD thy God: the LORD thy God hath chosen thee to be a special people unto himself, above all people that are upon the face of the earth." Why would God have done that? There were many other groups of people, and as history makes clear, no one group had been anymore dedicated to the one "true" God, than any other group. To the discerning mind, that Verse conveys this message: God did not love all of the children whom he had put on this Earth, and thus being, placed favor on only those whom He did love.

Deuteronomy, Chapters 8 through 11, basically convey the same messages as had been conveyed in the previous 7, and to the unbiased mind, there seems to be a conflict of interest in certain messages throughout those Chapters. First of all, why would the Lord choose to give of Himself, only to the Israelites, and no other group? Does that make any sense, when one takes into consideration the new covenant Jesus gave to His chosen Twelve, in Lection 76, Verse 5,

"A new commandment I give unto you, that ye love one another and all the creatures of God. Love is the fulfilling of the law. Love is of God, and God is love. Whoso loveth not, knoweth not God."

By the way, that is not a new Law, but an old, as Jesus made abundantly clear in Lection 46:24:
"This is the new Law unto the Israel of God, and the Law is within, for it is the Law of Love, and it is not new but old. Take heed that ye add nothing to this law, neither take anything from it. Verily I say unto you, they who believe and obey this law shall be saved, and they who know and obey it not, shall be lost."

73

In addition to the Law of Love, why would the Lord tell the Israelites, whom He had taken out of Egypt, and settled in Horeb: they had been there long enough; they were to go to other lands to possess them, by utterly destroying the men, women and children who possessed those lands, to the point none were left? Doesn't that contradict these Commandments: 6 – thou shall not kill; 8 - thou shall not steal; and 10 – thou shall not covet anything that belongs to your neighbor?

Could such an extreme act, truly be of God? It's not likely, especially when one considers the new, but old Commandment Jesus gave: A new commandment I give unto you, that ye love one another and all the creatures of God. Love is the fulfilling of the law. Love is of God, and God is love. Whoso loveth not, knoweth not God?

The source responsible for making such ungodly declarations, and such blood thirsty acts, as recorded in Deuteronomy, Chapters 1 through 11, comes to light in Chapter 12.

Verses 5 through 7:
5. But unto the place which the LORD your God shall choose out of all your tribes to put his name there, even unto his habitation shall ye seek, and thither thou shalt come:
6. And thither ye shall bring your burnt offerings, and your sacrifices, and your tithes, and heave offerings of your hand, and your vows, and your freewill offerings, and the firstlings of your herds and of your flocks:
7. And there ye shall eat before the LORD your God, and ye shall rejoice in all that ye put your hand unto, ye and your households, wherein the LORD thy God hath blessed thee.

And also in Verse 13 through 15

13. Take heed to thyself that thou offer not thy burnt offerings in every place that thou seest: 14. But in the place which the LORD shall choose in one of thy tribes, there thou shalt offer thy burnt offerings, and there thou shalt do all that I command thee. 15. Notwithstanding thou mayest kill and eat flesh in all thy gates, whatsoever thy soul lusteth after, according to the blessing of the LORD thy God which he hath given thee: the unclean and the clean may eat thereof, as of the roebuck, and as of the hart.

All of those Verses in Chapter 12, that I just read, revolve around the blood covenant of Exodus 24:8, and the blood sacrifice rituals and laws for the atonement of sin in Exodus 29:10-42, and as has been made clear through previous worship service homilies, the blood covenant is not of God. For the benefit of those who have not heard those homilies, please compare Isaiah 1:11-12, plus Jeremiah 7:22 and Daniel 8:11 and 9:27, to the blood covenant of Exodus 24, and the blood sacrifice rituals and laws of Exodus 29. In Isaiah, Chapter 1, Verses 11 and 12, the Lord wants to know who told the Israelites to do blood sacrifices. In Exodus, Chapters 24 and 29, we are told that Moses simply conveyed a commandment of the Lord, to do such, but obviously, it did not come from the Lord.

In addition, throughout His Gospel recorded by Apostle John, Jesus preached against the consumption of flesh, which solidifies the fact that Verse 27, wherein the Israelites are told, "thou shalt eat the flesh," is not of God, but of men, to suit their needs and traditions.

Brothers and Sisters, certain Deuteronomy lessons are absolutely of God, but those that violate His Law of love, are not. Whenever I read lessons within the Old Testament that contradict God's Law of Love, I always think about Verse 2, in Ezekiel, Chapter 18, "What mean ye, that ye use this proverb concerning the land of Israel, saying, The fathers have eaten sour grapes, and the children's teeth are set on edge?"

Children are born innocent, and that which they eventually become, is almost always based upon lessons given to them by their parents, and if the parents had bad experiences, eaten sour grapes, they are going to pass them on to their children, and they to their children. The Old Testament lessons that violate God's Law of Love, originate from one of two sources: the sour grapes passed on by parents to their children; or the 2nd, modifications by children of the wicked one, to God's Word, as it had been handed down to mankind, through the Holy Spirit.

Brother and Sisters, I once again implore that you become a warrior for God, His Son, and the Holy Spirit; don God's full armor, and share, through your love of your fellow Christians, God's true Word, and His Son's true Doctrine, that those whom you help, may also become warriors for God, His Son, and the Holy Spirit.

Chapter 12

Homily: A discussion of Leviticus 16 lessons as they relate to those taught by Jesus, as recorded by Apostle John.

Leviticus, Chapter 16, Verses 9 of today's Gospel reading, and 10 tell us about Aaron bringing a goat upon which the Lord's lot fell. The goat was to be a scapegoat for the atonement of sin. Next, Verse 11 tells us Aaron is to bring a bullock and kill it as a sin offering for himself and for his house. Then Verses 12 through 15 provide the instructions Aaron is to follow, regarding the bullock and goat, and last, Verse 16, declares, "And he shall make an atonement for the holy place, because of the uncleanness of the children of Israel, and because of their transgressions in all their sins: and so shall he do for the tabernacle of the congregation, that remaineth among them in the midst of their uncleanness."

There is much I want to talk about regarding those Verses, but first, Verse 16 contains scripture Jesus fulfilled, the first being, "And he shall make an atonement for the holy place." Jesus fulfilled that prophecy by making atonement for the Holy Place, known as the Temple, or the Sanctuary, in which blood sacrifices were carried out for the atonement of sin, by becoming the sacrifice to end the daily sacrifice.

Jesus' sacrifice on the cross, in-and-of-itself, did not end the daily sacrifice, but the sacrifices did end when Jesus, as He had done before His crucifixion, walked into the temple after His resurrection, on the day of the sacrifices, with a whip of seven cords, and drove the money changers out of the temple. The money changers had been frightened out of their wits, and immediately after that event, high priests started spreading disinformation about the event, and Jesus' crucifixion.

77

This is the second part of the scripture Jesus fulfilled: "so shall he do for the tabernacle of the congregation, that remaineth among them in the midst of their uncleanness." Jesus fulfilled that part before His crucifixion, as is revealed in these sections of Lection 71, Verses 2, 3 and 4: Verse 2, "He drove them all out of the temple," and in Verse 3, "Take these things hence; make not my Father's House an House of merchandise," and in Verse 4, "And he would not suffer that any man should carry any vessel of blood through the temple, or that any animals should be slain."

The lessons contained in Leviticus 16:9-16 all relate back to the blood covenant law Moses purportedly instituted in Exodus 24:8, and the blood sacrifice rituals and laws for the atonement of sin, in Exodus 29:10-42. Jesus preached against those laws throughout the Gospel of the Holy Twelve. I already mentioned one of the Verses in which he did, Verse 4, "And he would not suffer that any man should carry any vessel of blood through the temple, or that any animals should be slain."

However, the Gospel of the Holy Twelve does not contain the only proof which makes it clear Jesus would have preached against the blood covenant and the blood sacrifice rituals and laws, for such proof can also be found in the Old Testament through prophecies Jesus fulfilled. One of those prophecies is in Daniel 8:11, "Yea, he magnified himself even to the prince of the host, and by him the daily sacrifice was taken away;" these specific words, "and by him the daily sacrifice was taken away," confirm the fact that Jesus would have preached against the blood covenant, and the blood sacrifice rituals and laws for the atonement of sin, purportedly instituted by Moses.

Daniel 9:24 talks about the "transgression" that is stated in Leviticus 16:16, "and because of their transgressions in all their sins," which is addressed by this section of Daniel 9:24, "to finish the transgression, and to make an end of sins," and Daniel 9:25, makes clear Jesus is the "prince of the host," mentioned in Daniel 8, Verse 11, through this section of the Verse, "the commandment to restore and to build Jerusalem unto the Messiah the Prince."

Neither Daniel 9:24 or 25 tells us Jesus came to end the blood covenant and the blood sacrifice rituals and laws for the atonement of sin, but Verse 27 does, through these words, "in the midst of the week he shall cause the sacrifice and the oblation to cease." By the way, the Old Testament provides all the information needed to prove Jesus did end the sacrifice within the exact time frame as foretold, "in the midst of the week."

I want to share further proof Jesus came to repeal Moses' blood covenant law, and the sacrifice rituals and laws for the atonement for sin. John the Baptist told his followers in Lection 8, Verse 3, "The law was in part given by Moses, but grace and truth cometh in fullness by Jesus Christ," and in

Lection 25, Verse 8, which is part of Jesus' Sermon on the Mount, He said, "Behold One greater than Moses is here, and he will give you the higher law, even the perfect Law, and this Law shall ye obey," and in

Lection 30, Verse 5, Jesus said to His followers, "Verily, verily, I say unto you, Moses gave you not the true bread from heaven, but my Parent giveth you the true bread from heaven and the fruit of the living vine."

There is additional important evidence, making it clear Jesus preached against the blood covenant and the blood sacrifice rituals and laws for the atonement of sin, that I must bring to your attention: You likely picked up upon the fact that I mentioned twice: Moses *purportedly* instituted the blood covenant in Exodus 24:8 and the blood sacrifice rituals and laws for the atonement of sin with Exodus 29:10-42. In Lection 51, Verse 17, Jesus stated, "Against

79

Moses indeed I do not speak nor against the law, but against them who corrupted his law, which he permitted for the hardness of your hearts."

Further to that, the Lord told the Jews in Isaiah, Chapter 1, Verse 11, "To what purpose is the multitude of your sacrifices unto me? saith the LORD: I am full of the burnt offerings of rams, and the fat of fed beasts; and I delight not in the blood of bullocks, or of lambs, or of he goats;" and in Verse 12 He told them, "When ye come to appear before me, who hath required this at your hand, to tread my courts?"

Being the Lord told the Jews He did not want their blood sacrifices, and demanded to know who gave them the command to do such, and being Jesus made clear Moses' Law had been corrupted by men...the statements made by the Father, and the Son, make it clear the blood covenant in Exodus 24:8, and the blood sacrifice rituals and laws for the atonement of sin of Exodus 29:10-42, are by men to suit their needs and traditions, and they are *NOT* of God.

You now have proof that God's Word, as it had been handed down to mankind through Holy Spirit and the prophets, has been corrupted, and further to that, Jesus made it clear His Doctrine would also be corrupted when he told His Disciples in Lection 44, Verse 7, "But there shall arise after you, men of perverse minds who shall through ignorance or through craft, suppress many things which I have spoken unto you, and lay to me things which I never taught, sowing tares among the good wheat which I have given you to sow in the world."

In addition to that lesson, Jesus, in another lesson, told His chosen Twelve: the children of the wicked one would be responsible for sowing tares in the Doctrine He taught. Brothers and Sisters in Christ, I ask again, with all my heart, soul and mind: please be a warrior for God and His Son, and share with all those whom you feel you should, the lessons about God's and His Son's Truths, that I share with you in my homilies.

Sharing may not make you popular with certain people, or groups of people, and if that is a possibility, I encourage you to keep the following in mind: Jesus, because He preached against certain revered and longstanding Hebrew Laws, that had their beginnings in Genesis and Exodus, became very unpopular with certain Jews, and groups of Jews, and the fact He preached against their revered laws, is the factual reason Jesus suffered His crucifixion.

We today, do not have to be concerned with suffering the severe penalties that Jesus, His Apostles, and many of those whom were trained to preach Jesus' Doctrine, suffered. In conclusion, Jesus told His Twelve in Lection 73, Verse 10, "These things I command you, love one another and all the creatures of God. If the world hates you, know it hated me before you."

Chapter 13

Homily: a discussion of Ecclesiastes 3 lessons as they apply to Jesus' lessons taught as, recorded by Apostle John.

Brothers and Sisters in Christ, Ecclesiastes, Chapter 3, Verses 9 through 22, KJV, contains a few important lessons I want to bring to your attention, the first being in Verse 11, "he hath set the world in their heart, so that no man can find out the work that God maketh from the beginning to the end." Yes, the world is in our heart, and this world is all that we truly know; God's World, the Kingdom of Light, the Kingdom of Heaven, will remain a mystery to us till we pass over.

The second is in Verse 14, "I know that, whatsoever God doeth, it shall be for ever: nothing can be put to it, nor any thing taken from it.

Jesus told His Apostles in Lection 95, Verse 3: "I have set you as the light of the world, and as a city that cannot be hid. But the time cometh when darkness shall cover the earth, and gross darkness the people, and the enemies of truth and righteousness shall rule in my Name, and set up a kingdom of this world, and oppress the peoples, and cause the enemy to blaspheme, putting for my doctrines the opinions of men, and teaching in my Name that which I have not taught, and darkening much that I have taught by their traditions;" and in

Verse 4, "But be of good cheer, for the time will also come when the truth they have hidden shall be manifested, and the light shall shine, and the darkness shall pass away, and the true kingdom shall be established which shall be in the world, but not of it."

Verse 4 certainly agrees with, and drives home the fact that this statement in Ecclesiastes, Chapter 3, Verse 14, "whatsoever God doeth, it shall be for ever: nothing can be put to it, nor any thing taken from it," is in deed a fact.

The last lesson within in Ecclesiastes, Chapter 3, Verses 9 through 22, is contained in Verses 19 and 20:

Verse 19, "For that which befalleth the sons of men befalleth beasts; even one thing befalleth them: as the one dieth, so dieth the other; yea, they have all one breath; so that a man hath no preeminence above a beast: for all is vanity;" and

Verse 20, "All go unto one place; all are of the dust, and all turn to dust again."

Verse 19 tells us beasts and men come from the same breath, and Verse 20 declares that men and beasts all return to the same place, and that all are of dust, and return to dust. Those two statements are very profound, for they are confirmed by Jesus in Lection 34, Verse 9, when He said to the people, after they accused Him of caring for, and loving creatures, like they were His brothers and sisters, "Verily these are your fellow creatures of the great Household of God, yea, they are your brethren and sisters, having the same breath of life in the Eternal."

"The same breath of the life of the eternal" certainly coincides with Ecclesiastes, Chapter 3, Verse 19, wherein it is stated, "yea, they have all one breath."

Jesus made another very profound statement in Lection 34, Verse 10, when He said "And whosoever careth for one of the least of these, and giveth it to eat and drink in its need, the same doeth it unto me, and whoso willingly suffereth one of these to be in want, and defendeth it not when evilly entreated, suffereth the evil as done unto me, FOR AS YE HAVE DONE IN THIS LIFE, SO SHALL IT BE DONE UNTO YOU IN THE LIFE TO COME."

That last section of Verse 10, "FOR AS YE HAVE DONE IN THIS LIFE, SO SHALL IT BE DONE UNTO YOU IN THE LIFE TO COME," is most profound and revealing, as it's a very serious eye opener to those who can see and hear, for Jesus made it clear through that statement, souls experience more than one lifetime.

Actually, Jesus preached that fact many times in Lections throughout the Gospel of the Holy Twelve, and He often told His chosen Twelve, and His followers, souls experience births, deaths and rebirths many times, until they reach the purification required to enter into the Kingdom of Heaven. But He also stated that those souls who refuse to amend their ways to those of God, will eventually be utterly destroyed; I should note at this point that Jesus did not preach a sinning soul would spend all of eternity in hell.

Verses 4 through 6 of Lection 34, also contain a very important and clarifying lesson that relates to another in the Gospel of the Holy Twelve: In those Verses Jesus blessed the fig tree that gave him and the women with him shelter and shade, and it flourished thereafter. In Lection 70, Verses 1 through 6, Peter, when leaving Bethany, came upon a fig tree when he was hungry, and because it had no fruit on it, he cursed it. The next day, when Jesus, Peter and the other Disciples passed the fig tree, Peter saw that it was flourishing, and asked Jesus why, when he, Peter, had cursed it the day before. Jesus chastised him in a benevolent fatherly way for cursing the fig tree, and explained why the tree still flourished.

However, that story within the New Testament, is told differently, which is in Matthew, Chapter 21, Verses 18 through 21, KJV. When one reads those Verses they will find that when leaving Bethany, it is stated that Jesus cursed a fig tree for not having fruit on it, and the tree withered away. Matthew, Chapter 21, Verses 18 through 21, creates a vindictive image of Jesus, while Lection 70,

Verses 1 through 6, clearly demonstrate a very loving and caring person. That certainly is a distinct difference in character portrayal between the writings of Apostle John, which were found by Catholic priests in 1870, and the authorized doctrine contained in the King James and Catholic Bibles; to those who can see and hear, it is a clear example of the corruption by men to suit their needs and traditions, which Jesus foretold to His chosen Twelve, would happen.

As I already mentioned, Jesus told us in Lection 95, Verse 4, "But be of good cheer, for the time will also come when the truth they have hidden shall be manifested, and the light shall shine, and the darkness shall pass away, and the true kingdom shall be established which shall be in the world, but not of it."

Brothers and Sisters in Christ, the time has come that Jesus foretold of in Verse 4, for I am one of many who have been anointed to bring God's and His Son's Truths to the world, and I ask you to please join us; become a warrior for God and Jesus, wearing the full armor of God, and share Their Truths with those who have the eyes to see, and the ears to hear.

Chapter 14

Homily: A discussion of Micah Verses as they related to lessons Jesus taught, as they were written by Apostle John.

Brother and Sisters, there are a few Verses within today's reading of Micah that I wish to address, and Jesus' Gospel written by Apostle John. Micah Chapter 4, Verse 1, told us the mountain of the house of the LORD shall be established in the top of the mountains, and it shall be exalted above the hills; and people shall flow unto it. Then Verse 2 told us the people should go up to the mountain of the LORD, and learn of his ways, and walk in his paths, for the law shall go forth of Zion, and the word of the LORD from Jerusalem.

Zion is a mountain near Jerusalem, and Micah 4:1-2, prophesied the people will flow to it, and there they will learn the word, the law, and Jesus, who is the Lord from Jerusalem, fulfilled that prophecy. Once the people have learned, they shall go forth from Zion and tell it to others. By the way, I want to make clear that scholars do not believe Zion is the place where Jesus gave His Sermon on the Mount.

Micah Chapter 5, Verses 1 through 4, also provide prophecy which Jesus fulfilled. Verse 1 told us, "He hath laid siege against us: they shall smite the judge of Israel with a rod upon the cheek." How did Jesus, Judge of Israel, lay siege to it? Apostle John, when recording His Master's Doctrine, wrote frequently the fact that Jesus preached against the daily sacrifice, yet that reality is only accounted for in the Old Testament, within the Daniel 8:11 and 9:27 prophecies, wherein it is foretold the Messiah the Prince will end the daily sacrifice. Being Jesus preached against the revered Hebrew blood sacrifice rituals and laws of Exodus 29:10-42, is the manner in which He fulfilled prophecy, and laid siege to Israel.

Why did Jesus come into the world to do such? The answer lies in the Book of Isaiah, Chapter 1, Verses 11 and 12, wherein the Lord made it clear to Isaiah the blood covenant of Exodus, Chapter 24:8, and the blood sacrifice rituals and laws of Exodus 29:10-42, are not of Him, but of men to suit their needs and traditions.

Jesus also laid siege to Israel by preaching against cruelty to animals, and those lessons He preached complimented the lesson within Ecclesiastes, Chapter 3, Verses 19 and 20, wherein we are told that beasts came from the same breath of the eternal, as mankind.

There's also another part of Verse 1 which Jesus fulfilled: "they shall smite the judge of Israel with a rod upon the cheek." Smite Jesus they did, when Pilate ordered Him to be scourged before being crucified.

Jesus also fulfilled Micah 5, Verse 2, "But thou, Bethlehem Ephratah, though thou be little among the thousands of Judah, yet out of thee shall he come forth unto me that is to be ruler in Israel." We all know Jesus was born in Bethlehem, which fulfilled the first part of Verse 2. The second part, "yet out of thee shall he come forth unto me that is to be ruler in Israel," was fulfilled thru Lection 2, Verse 5, "And the Lord God shall give unto him the throne of his father David: and he shall reign over the house of Jacob forever."

Micah 5, Verse 3 told us, "Then the remnant of his brethren shall return unto the children of Israel." Jesus fulfilled that prophecy when after His resurrection He told His Apostles in Lection 88, Verse 6, to first preach His Doctrine in Jerusalem.

And it should go without saying that Jesus also fulfilled Micah 5, Verse 4, which stated, "He shall be great unto the ends of the earth."

Next I want to address a section of Verse 6 within Lection 2, from the reading of the Gospel of the Holy Twelve, for it is extremely important. That important section reads, "That holy thing which shall be born of thee shall be called the Christ, the Child of God, and his Name on earth shalt be called Jesu-Maria, for he shall save the people from their sins, whosoever shall repent and obey his Law."

Everyone knows, or should know this part about Jesus, "he shall save the people from their sins." However, most of those who are Jesus' followers, do not know about this part of Gabriel's statement to Mary, for it is not in the New Testament: "whosoever shall repent and obey his Law." In fulfillment of the Jeremiah 31:31 prophecy, Jesus gave mankind new laws, many of which were contrary to Hebrew Law, and being they contradicted revered Hebrew Law, which supports the reason taught by Pharisee Saul/Paul that Jesus had been crucified, they are not found within the New Testament.

Jesus taught that mankind had been given a ladder with many steps that had to be followed in order to achieve the purification required to enter into the Kingdom of Heaven, and made it very clear that repentance and amendment were the only methods by which sins against God's Laws could be remitted. Contrary to the belief of many Christians, Jesus did not preach He would be a sacrifice to redeem mankind from their sins, nor are there any Old Testament prophecies that foretell such, even though many Christians mistakenly believe there are.

Brothers and Sisters in Christ, again, I humbly ask you, with all of my heart, soul and mind, to be a warrior for God and His Son, and I ask that you share Their Truths which I share with you. Jesus stated in His Sermon on the Mount, "behold One greater than Moses is here, and he [Jesus] will give you the higher law, even the perfect Law, and this Law shall ye obey. Whosoever therefore shall break one of these commandments which he [Jesus] shall give, and shall

88

teach men so, they shall be called the least in the kingdom; but whosoever shall do, and teach them, the same shall be called great in the kingdom of Heaven."

Brothers and Sisters, I call upon you to be a teacher of God's, and His Son's Truths, and "be called great in the kingdom of Heaven."

Chapter 15

Homily: Discussion of Jeremiah lessons as they apply to lessons Jesus' taught, as recorded by Apostle John, and those preached by Pharisee Saul/Paul, and adopted as authorized church doctrine by the First Council of Nicaea 325 AD.

Brothers and Sisters in Christ, today's reading of Jeremiah, Chapter 7, Verses 19 through 31, contained a few very important lessons, which tie directly with lessons Jesus taught often in His Gospel recorded by Apostle John. Verses 19 and 20 make it clear the Lord is upset when He told Jeremiah: the Israelites anger Me, and My fury shall be poured out; and in Verse 21 the Lord told Jeremiah, they are to put their burnt offerings in their sacrifices. The Lord clarified His statement in Verse 22, when He said, "For I spake not unto your fathers, nor commanded them in the day that I brought them out of the land of Egypt, concerning burnt offerings or sacrifices."

Jesus preached often against burnt offerings and sacrifices, which fulfilled the Daniel 8:11 prophecy that foretold He would end the daily sacrifice, and the Daniel 9:27 prophecy foretold when He would do such. During today's reading of the Gospel of the Holy Twelve, Lection 51, you heard an excellent example of the burnt offering and sacrifice lessons Jesus preached, in Verse 15, when He said, "As also Jeremiah bear witness when he saith, concerning blood offerings and sacrifices, I the Lord God commanded none of these things in the day that ye came out of Egypt."

Jesus, in fulfillment of the Jeremiah Chapter 31, Verse 31 prophecy, did give mankind new laws, one of them being the law I just addressed, which negated the revered Hebrew blood covenant of Exodus 24, and blood sacrifice laws of Exodus 29. Actually, that law was not the only law He gave that contradicted revered Hebrew Laws within Exodus and Genesis. In addition, Jesus gave to mankind the steps a soul

90

must follow and obey to earn its salvation, and they contradicted lessons within Pharisee Saul/Paul's epistles in the New Testaments of the King James and Catholic Bibles.

Unfortunately, none of the Laws Jesus preached in fulfillment of the Jeremiah 31:31 prophecy, which were contradictory to Hebrew Law, are found in the New Testament, and neither are the steps a soul must follow to earn its salvation. The steps Jesus taught to earn salvation, contradicted Hebrew Law. Why is that so? The path to salvation, according to Hebrew Law, was accomplished through the bloody sacrifices, which were done in accordance with the blood sacrifice rituals and laws of Exodus 29:10-42, for the atonement of sin.

Jeremiah, Chapter 7, Verse 24, told us, "But they [the Jews when they were led out of Egypt] hearkened not, nor inclined their ear, but walked in the counsels and in the imagination of their evil heart, and went backward, and not forward." God sent His Son, Christ Jesus, to again bring the Jews forward by correcting the corruption to His Word, which had been handed down to mankind through Holy Spirit and prophets, and in fulfillment of scripture, Jesus did exactly that.

However, history makes it very clear that Pharisee Saul/Paul diligently worked to keep the Jews backward, as he had been a staunch protector of the blood sacrifice rituals and laws, purportedly instituted by Moses in Exodus 29. In so doing, Saul/Paul caused countless future Christians to also be backward, as were the Israelites after coming out of Egypt.

The Lord drove home in Jeremiah 7, Verse 25, the fact He had been trying hard to eliminate the blood covenant of Exodus 24, and the sacrifice laws of Exodus 29, when He said, "Since the day that your fathers came forth out of the land of Egypt unto this day, I have even sent unto you all my servants the prophets, daily rising up early and sending them." And Jesus solidified His Father did such, in Lection 52, Verse 6, when He told the Jews, "The All Holy hath sent you many prophets, but ye rose against them that were contrary to your lusts, reviling some and slaying others." What lust had Jesus been referring to? It had been the daily blood sacrifices as prescribed in Exodus 29, for the atonement of sin.

Biblical writings, in addition to the Old Testaments of the King James and Catholic Bibles, and the Gospel of the Holy Twelve, also crystallize the fact the blood covenant of Exodus 24, and the blood sacrifice rituals and laws of Exodus 29, are not of God, but of men to suit their needs and traditions. One such writing is The Clementine Homilies. The Clementine Homilies, written by early Church Father, Clement of Rome, contains an epistle from Apostle Peter to James, Bishop of Jerusalem, who is Jesus' Brother, and it also contains a record of the doctrine Apostle Peter preached. Peter personally trained Clement of Rome in Jesus' Doctrine, and appointed him to be a Church Father.

The messages of the lessons Apostle Peter preached, as they were recorded by Clement of Rome, mirror the messages of the lessons Jesus preached, as they were recorded by Apostle John. These writings, separately, and combined with the Old Testaments of the King James and Catholic Bibles, solve beyond a shadow of a doubt, the glaring contradictions between Exodus, Chapters 24 and 29, and the Books of Isaiah, Chapter 1, and Jeremiah, Chapter 7, and Daniel, Chapters 8 and 9.

For instance, two Verses within the Gospel of the Holy Twelve, provide definitive, supporting evidence, that makes clear which Exodus / Isaiah lessons that contradict each other, are of God, and those that are of men. The first Verse is 17, of Lection 51, when Jesus told the Pharisees, priests and scribes, "against Moses indeed I do not speak nor against the law, but against them who corrupted his law, which he permitted for the hardness of your hearts."

Being we know the Lord sent prophets, and His Son, to eliminate the blood sacrifices, Verse 17 of Lection 51, adds to the mountain of evidence which indicates the blood covenant of Exodus 24, and the blood sacrifice rituals and laws for the atonement of sin within Exodus 29, are of men.

Then, in Lection 64, Verse 11, Jesus stated, "Verily I say unto you, my twelve whom I have chosen, *that which hath been taught by them of old time* is true—though corrupted by the foolish imaginations of men."

That which hath been taught by them of old time had been the Gospel of Jesus' time, and today, is known as our Old Testament.

The next important lesson of Jeremiah 7, is contained in Verse 28, "This is a nation that obeyeth not the voice of the LORD their God, nor receiveth correction: truth is perished, and is cut off from their mouth." Jesus made clear the Lord's Truth had in fact been cut off from their mouth, when He said in Verse 14, of Lection 51, "Ye hypocrites, well did Esaias speak of you, and your forefathers, sayings This people draweth nigh unto Me, with their mouths, and honour me with their lips, but their heart is far from me, for in vain do they worship Me teaching and believing, and teaching for divine doctrines, the commandments of men in my name but to satisfy their own lusts."

The blood covenant of Exodus 24, and the blood sacrifice rituals and law for the atonement of sin in Exodus 29, are among those divine doctrines of men, that are taught in God's Name, which Jesus spoke of.

We have another important lesson in Jeremiah 7, Verse 30, which states, "For the children of Judah have done evil in my sight, saith the LORD: they have set their abominations

93

in the house which is called by my name, to pollute it." In Lection 49, Verse 6, Jesus told the scribes, "It is written in the prophets, My house shall be called a house of prayer for all nations, for the sacrifice of praise and thanksgiving. But ye have made it a house of slaughter and filled it with abominations."

Jesus, in fulfillment of scripture, did all that had been foretold, in an effort to bring the Jews forward; He constantly preached against the daily sacrifice for the remission of sin, and that, as biblical history makes clear, is the actual reason the Jews demanded His crucifixion.

Jesus preached often this statement in today's reading of Lection 51, Verse 18, "But, behold, a greater than Moses is here," and as an example, He stated in Lection 25, Verse 8, which is from His Sermon on the Mount, "But behold One greater than Moses is here, and he will give you the higher law, even the perfect Law, and this Law shall ye obey."

I have already mentioned the fact that the laws Jesus gave in fulfillment of the Jeremiah 31:31 prophecy, that were contradictory to Hebrew Law, are not in the New Testament, and history crystallizes the fact Roman Emperor Constantine had been instrumental in bringing that about. Constantine convened and presided over the First Council of Nicaea, 325 AD, and history makes it clear that when conspiring with Orthodox Nicene Bishops, he had exerted his influence to sway the Council to adopt the doctrine that had been preached by Pharisee Saul/Paul, over the doctrine that had been preached by Jesus, His Apostles, and all those whom they trained.

A mountain of biblical evidence supports that statement, and a significant factor is this: after the Council adjourned, it is recorded in history that Constantine ordered the destruction of any doctrine that was contrary to that which had been authorized by the Council. By the way, biblical history tells us Constantine, through his participation in the

First Council of Nicaea 325 AD, set the precedent for future Emperors to exert influence within the Church.

Jesus prophesied to His chosen Twelve that His Doctrine would be changed and things would be taught in His Name that He did not teach, and Pharisee Saul/Paul certainly fulfilled that prophecy. Pharisee Saul/Paul preached doctrine that had been structured to maintain the integrity of the revered blood covenant of Exodus, Chapter 24, Verse 8, and longstanding blood sacrifice rituals and laws of Exodus 29:10-42, through craft, which Jesus foretold would be utilized. Pharisee Saul/Paul craftily glossed over the factual intent of his doctrine, which had been to preserve the revered Hebrew Laws of Exodus 24 and 29, by mixing it with doctrine Jesus had actually taught.

Further to that, Jesus knew such would happen when He told His chosen Twelve in Lection 89:9, "And yet another shall arise and *he shall teach many things which I have taught* you already, and he shall spread the Gospel among the Gentiles with great zeal. But the keys of the Kingdom will I give to those who succeed thee in my Spirit *and obeying my law*. There are two sections of Verse 9 that are important: the first being, "*he shall teach many things which I have taught;*" Pharisee Saul/Paul did teach many things Jesus taught, which as I mentioned, had been done through craft to disguise his real intent; and the second is, "*and obeying my law.*" Pharisee Saul/Paul did not obey Jesus' Law, and thus could not receive the keys to the Kingdom.

Documented history makes it clear Jesus' Apostles, and all those whom were initiated into the Christhood, continued to preach Jesus' Doctrine after His Crucifixion, and that is the factual reason Pharisee Saul/Paul staunchly hunted, persecuted, and was directly responsible for the imprisonment, and/or deaths, of many of those who preached and/or believed in Jesus' Doctrine. Those who preached His Doctrine, plus His followers, became known as the Jewish Christian Movement.

It is important to understand the craft that had been employed to protect the blood covenant: Pharisee Saul/Paul, or someone, through disinformation, created the myth that Jesus' death on the cross had been a blood sacrifice to redeem mankind from their sins, and that disinformation melded perfectly with the blood sacrifice laws of Exodus 29, for the atonement of sin.

Jesus steadfastly preached that a soul must earn its way into the Kingdom of Heaven, and never once did He preach He would suffer, and be a sacrifice to redeem all of mankind from their sins, nor do any Old Testament prophecies foretell such. Many claim the Isaiah 53 prophecies state the Messiah would suffer for all mankind, but when one studies those prophecies with a discerning and unbiased mind, they find that His suffering had been only for the Israelites, and no other nation.

In closing, Jesus told His Apostles in Lection 95, Verses 3 and 4, "I have set you as the light of the world, and as a city that cannot be hid. But the time cometh when darkness shall cover the earth, and gross darkness the people, and the enemies of truth and righteousness shall rule in my Name, and set up a kingdom of this world, and oppress the peoples, and cause the enemy to blaspheme, putting for my doctrines the opinions of men, and teaching in my Name that which I have not taught, and darkening much that I have taught by their traditions. But be of good cheer, for the time will also come when the truth they have hidden shall be manifested, and the light shall shine, and the darkness shall pass away, and the true kingdom shall be established which shall be in the world, but not of it."

As disciples of Christ, I encourage you to share His truth with many, and help make a reality in this electronic age of information sharing, His statement, "for the time will also come when the truth they have hidden shall be manifested, and the light shall shine, and the darkness shall pass away."

Be a warrior for God and His Son, and be a warrior for your fellow Christians, who believe they have been saved, because of Pharisee Saul/Paul's counterfeit teachings; share with them the Truths I share with you, that they may know that which they must do to earn their salvation, that has been hidden from them, due to the efforts of Pharisee Saul/Paul. It's a shame that the conspiracy between Constantine and Orthodox Nicene Bishops, worked, for their combined efforts resulted in the doctrine preached by Saul/Paul, being adopted as authorized church doctrine, over that of the Jewish Christian Movement. It is my opinion, that as a group, they are directly responsible for stealing true Christianity from mankind.

"Dreams & Visions
of God's Anointed Prophets
& Two Witnesses"

Russell and Paul Maddock

Chapter 16

The Anointing of Russell and Paul Maddock as God's Prophets and Two Witnesses

Prophets within the Old Testament were given wideawake visions and dreams, many of which became prophecies that Jesus fulfilled during His lifetime, with most occurring during His Messianic Ministry. Russell and Paul Maddock are two such modern day prophets, for some visions and dreams they have been given, have already come to pass.

Russell Maddock

Hello again Rev. Davis. I wanted to send what I wrote down shortly after my experience back in Feb 1993. I also want to say what a blessing your website is. My brother and I have never come across anyone who understands and teaches the way you do.

We both come across the Gospel of the Holy Twelve several years ago. We bought many books and gave them to people who seemed to be open to the true teachings of Christ. There is no doubt that God has called you and anointed you for that purpose. Right from the beginning, the Holy Spirit was telling us there were problems with what we knew as Christianity.

For many years, all we had was the King James Bible to try and understand why God was telling us they worship Me under false pretenses. But, at that time I did not know what those false pretenses were. So, with that said, I would like to share with you, the experience I had some 21 years ago. The e-mail I sent yesterday was filled with so many miss spelled words, I felt I needed to find what I wrote down shortly after what took place, and copy it with all the right spelling.

I pray what I feel God has inspired me to do, will go forth and accomplish what God has intended. May God and His Son be praised. This paper I am sitting down to write, is about a supernatural experience that was from the Lord Almighty God. This experience took place in the living room of my home. I will explain it the best way I can in my own words.

Approximately three weeks after I surrendered my life over to Jesus Christ as my Lord and Saviour, the Holy Spirit of God was ministering to my spirit while I was working on my job. God's Spirit was telling me that when I got home, I was to remove all the unclean things that were in my house, and to place them outside of my home. I knew exactly what those things were. I still had in my home, beer bottles, rock and roll albums, marijuana paraphernalia and pornographic magazines. All these things were a part of my life before I made Jesus my Lord. The Lord said it was time to clean house! I knew exactly what I was to do, when I got home from work.

As soon as I got home, I grabbed some paper bags and started filling them up with all the unclean things. Then, I placed all of the bags outside of the house as I was instructed to do. After that was done, I went about my normal routine that one does after a full day of work. With all of this out of the way, I sat down to read the bible. As I was reading the word, God's presence was so very strong. So, I put down the bible to seek the Lord.

In my living room, I had an old bench press that I would use as my altar. But, before I knelt to pray, I turned off all the lights. The house was completely dark, except for the street light coming through the curtains that faced north. I had no idea what was about to happen, because I had been doing this same thing nearly every night since coming to know the Lord.

When I knelt to pray, the instant my knees touched the floor, I was struck with power from on High, that words cannot express, nor explain! The best I can tell you........It was like being plugged into a wall socket! This supernatural power was so awesome. The instant the power struck me, my hands flew straight up, my head was flung back, and my back was arched. The power from on High, was in me....around me....through me to the point, I thought my body was going to explode from the intense power that was passing through my body.

During all of this, I was in an uncontrollable time of praise and worship of the Lord Jesus Christ. I can remember I could not tell Jesus I loved Him enough!!! The feeling of love was so very strong. That is why at no time was I afraid or alarmed at what was taking place. And, as if this was not enough?? Seconds after it all started, passing in front of me, were two huge beings. I knew they were there, because when they passed in front of the window, they blocked the light. All I could see was their outlines. There was no doubt they were there!

My ceilings are eight foot or more, and they were just as tall. One was about a foot above the other in height. Their shoulders were as wide as a yard stick. I knew this, because as they glided past, they both were facing me, and were very close to one another as well. From what I could tell, they both seem to be wearing gown like clothing, with a sash at their waist. The taller one had attire upon his head like a priest would wear. And, the other one was wearing what also looked like a helmet with a large spike protruding from the top. Since they only blocked the light one time, I assumed they only glided around me one time. That was enough to let me know they were there.

Their presence lingered for two hours or more. I was soaking wet with sweat after it was all over. What a wonderfully amazing experience it was. I will never forget it! Even when I awoke the next morning, I could still feel their presence, but not nearly as strong. I was so excited it was hard to contain myself through the day. I knew God had touched me in a very special way. It all began for me after that wonderful evening. My search for why and what purpose was those two sent? And, who were they??

My brother is going to send you his experience that took place about three months after mine. He too had seen the two glide around him as well. When you read about what the Lord showed him, you will understand why I felt what I did within my body. His experience was more visual, mine was more physical. The Lord has told us we are like a coin that has two sides, and yet are one.

To God be All the Glory. Amen and Amen. God bless you Rev. Davis. You are truly doing a great and wonderful work for the Kingdom of God. Your ministry which God has called you to do, has now become my church. Thank you for answering God's calling upon your life. What a blessing it has, and will be to many many people. To the Holy Parent and Son be all the Glory. Amen.

Paul Maddock

God anointed me in the late summer of 1993. Anoint means to pour oil upon, to consecrate. The word consecrate means; to make or declare to be sacred, by ceremonies or rites; to appropriate to sacred uses; to set apart, dedicate, or devote to the service and worship of God. To render venerable; to make respected; as customs or principles consecrated by time, to devote to a sacred or high purpose; to hallow.

This super natural act of God upon my life has dramatically changed me forever. Even now, when I think about it I am amazed by His great power, mercy and love.

I was in one of the most difficult times of my life when God chose to anoint me. I was going through a dreadful divorce from my wife of six years. I found out that she was unfaithful to me and broke the covenant of marriage between us by having an affair with another man. We have a son that was four years old at the time. God has taught me much about the condition of many of His people by this painful experience. It has been a great spiritual awakening to me, and hope and pray it will be to you also. Let me tell you about it.

I was on my knees in prayer before God one night about midnight. I was crying out to Him to help me get through this divorce. That day I had seen my lawyer and I told him about my wife's car being at her boy friends house at five in the morning. I had seen it on my way to work. She had just moved out a few days before. I was greatly troubled because I had no idea where my son was. My lawyer said there is nothing I can do because this is a no fault divorce.

As I was crying out to the Lord in prayer that night, I said "Lord, I give you my whole life, my whole life!" Suddenly, with my eyes closed, a small window appeared about five feet above me. The window was slightly two feet to my left and was about the size of a sheet of typing paper. It was closed but I could see light coming from the seams of the window.

I was facing north on my knees in prayer by my sofa, in front of a big picture window in my living room. Then the Lord took me out of my body and across the other side of the room. I was about twelve feet away from my body, which was now shown to me as semi-transparent. Inside my body was shown to me a large white vessel. Its shape was wide at the mouth area and narrower at the neck, with a wide and larger base. There was a bluish white aura all around it, and the color of the vessel was the most radiant white, the same white light that was coming from the seams of the small window above me.

This white light was very bright but in no way did it ever hurt my eyes. The large vessel that was inside me was from the top of my head to the lowest part of my groin area. Then the Lord took me by His Spirit and elevated me off the floor and over my body with the vessel inside. It was then that the Lord began to lower me down inside the empty vessel and turn me clock- ways, ever so slowly so that I could see how clean and spotless it was.

The vessel inside reminded me of a thermos bottle, which was metallic looking down in. The light was also within the vessel. Then the Lord brought me back out from the vessel counter clock-ways and placed me back inside my body. I could now see the closed window above me; the inside as well as the outside of the vessel which was inside my semi-transparent body. I could also see the surrounding room all at the same time. Then the Lord opened up the small window above me, and out came a controlled stream of crystal clear oil in about a three inch diameter stream which was being directed right toward my head from the window above me.

The stream of oil had a slight arch to it as it approached my head from the window above. And just before the oil reached me, my head was tilted back by the Holy Spirit of God, and He began to fill my vessel. Now I could see that there was thee shapes of precious stones in the oil also. The stones were clear crystal and three different sizes, and the light was in the stones also. The first shape was in the shape of a rectangle and about three inches tall, one and a half inches wide and one half inch thick, with many precise cuttings. This stone was very majestic looking.

The second stone was in the shape of two triangles base to base, with its two smallest points at the top and bottom. Its size was two and one half inches tall and its widest part was its center, which was about one and one fourth inches wide.

The third shape was in the shape of a hexagon, which was about the size of my ring finger nail, and its thickness was about one quarter of an inch. All the stones were three-dimensional. I would say there was about one half gallon of these three shapes of crystal stones, mixed in with the oil within the vessel.

The stream of oil did not stop until the vessel was filled to its fullest point, without running over. Not even one drop of the crystal clear oil was spilled during the whole duration of time it took to fill my vessel. After the stream of oil stopped, I saw the Glory of the Lord that was poured into my vessel, for a period of time, which I would say, was about three minutes.

The crystal stones and clear liquid moved in a constant rhythmic motion. Because now in the bottom of the vessel was shown to me a spring which came from the bottom of the vessel. I was completely struck by the beauty of the Lord's Holiness, which was being shown to me. The color was like looking through a prism with the sun shining through it. All the colors of the rainbow was there. The color of the covenant of God.

Then the light of the moon which shown through the large picture window, was blocked out four a split second as something moved by it. It was then that I noticed these two large beings pass by the window in front of me. I saw their silhouettes as they glided in a full circle around the living room, counter clock-ways. They were at least seven feet tall, with one being a little taller than the other.

The taller of the two was wearing the type of head attire that a priest would were. And the second one was wearing what looked like a helmet that a warrior would wear. They were shoulder to shoulder as they circled me.

My brother Russell, who was anointed a short time before me, saw the same two angels in his living room. I truly was in another dimension at this time. All these things I saw at the same time. I have described them to the best of my ability.

After the two large angels made a full circle around me in the living room, I was back in the physical state. All that was shown to me disappeared including the small window. Immediately I heard the Lord speak to me saying, "What I have given you will never leave unless you turn your back on me and walk away. Then I will take it as quickly as I have given it unto you. I am going to restore all your losses and then some."

My wife had left me and took my son and most of our possessions. The house was empty. In many of the dreams and visions the Holy Spirit has showed this to be a condition of the heart within the church in the last day generation of the Fig Tree. Much of the church has listened to the spirit of a counterfeit christ, and has embraced the lie. The Lord calls that part of the church that believes this false doctrine "the Defiled Bride." The spiritual place in which she dwells is called Babylon.

Much of the church in this last day generation is in Babylon, which means Babel or confusion toward the TRUTH of God's Word. The Lord spoke to me these words just after He said I am going to restore all your losses and then some;" Move when I tell you to move, and stay when I tell you to stay. Do not go before me and do not lag behind."

The Lord's holy Spirit has taught us this great TRUTH, because the Lord is the authority of all TRUTH. My son represents the children who have been raised up and taught in Babylon. By the Great Harlot, the Defiled Bride, his mother, who ran after another lover. The Defiled Bride which is the church that has embraced another lover's words as truth has taught the child, the doctrine of Babylon.

But the Lord is fighting for his children. By His mighty Holy Spirit, in the name of His genuine Son Jesus Christ, through His Anointed ones, He will bring the children out of Spiritual Babylon. I then asked the Lord about the two beings my brother and I had seen in our living rooms. It was then that the Holy Spirit spoke to my spirit, telling me to go to Zachariah chapter 3 and 4.

As I began to read in God's Word about Joshua and Zerubbabel, the Spirit told me that this is the likeness of the two anointed ones. The rebirth of the Fig Tree represents the rebirth of the Spiritual Israel. This is none other than the true church of Jesus Christ. The true Bride of Christ.

In Zechariah 3:1-7, the Lord chose Joshua to govern his house. And we see how Satan the accuser, tries to oppress Joshua the High Priest, but is rebuked by the Lord. Then the Lord causes Joshua's iniquity to pass from him.

The command and promise to Joshua from God is in 3:7-8. Thus saith the Lord of host; If thou wilt walk in My ways, and if thou wilt keep My charge, then thou shalt also judge My house, and shalt also keep My courts, and I will give thee places to walk among these that stand by. Hear now, O Joshua the high priest, thou, and thy fellows that sit before thee: for they are men wondered at: for behold; I will bring forth My Servant the BRANCH.

This Branch is none other than Christ Himself. And who are these fellows or colleagues; men wondered at, men to serve as signs of one greater? Remember the Holy Spirit said that this was the likeness of the anointing.

Let us continue in 3: 9-10. For behold the stone that I have laid before Joshua; upon one stone shall be seven eyes: Behold, I will engrave the graving thereof, saith the lord of hosts, and I will remove the iniquity of that land in one day.

In that day, saith the Lord of hosts, shall ye call every man his neighbor under the vine and under the fig tree.

The Lord showed Joshua the second coming of Christ, and how it would be ushered in by the men of signs: men to serve as signs of one greater, which is Christ himself. This will bring in the 1000-Year Millennium upon the earth.

The Lord showed Joshua and wanted him to know how he was included in His great plan, for he was chosen to rebuild the temple that was ravaged by Nebuchadnezzar the king of Babylon. The foundation of the first temple, which Solomon built, was still there and that foundation is TRUTH.

Now Joshua who was born in Babylon, which is the likeness of spiritual confusion, is chosen by God to lead in the rebuilding of the second temple, which is the very temple in which Christ the Lamb of God would stand and speak the TRUTH.

Now as we look at Zechariah 4:1, where God is speaking about Zerubbabel. The angel of God is sent from heaven to Zechariah to encourage His people to work and rebuild the temple of God. The first temple was ravaged and the people spent years in Babylon because of their rebellious hearts toward God's Word.

In Zechariah 4:2 he is shown one candlestick which is symbolic of the covenant with God toward man.

In Revelation 11:4 is the symbolic meaning of the two covenants, the old and the new. The two anointed ones are shown to be here in flesh bodies, during the time span of the second covenant, which was brought in by the death and resurrection of Christ. This takes place just before Christ's second return. They speak with the powerful anointing of the Holy Spirit, with the TRUTH they have been given by God to lead the children out of spiritual Babylon. To prepare a holy Bride for Christ soon to return.

The candlestick spoken of in Zechariah 4:2 is a golden stand with seven individual lit candles on it. The number seven is symbolic of God's spiritual perfection.

Zechariah 4:2-3 speaks about the spiritual meaning of the two Anointed Ones, which are shown as two Olive Trees. From the olive trees comes the oil which is symbolic of the Holy Spirit's TRUTH that fills the bowl. Then the oil travels down seven golden pipes toward the seven candlesticks, which are all on one stand. It is the oil, which keeps the candles burning. Without oil, that is to say TRUTH, the candle goes out.

Zechariah 4:4-5. So I answered and spoke to the angel that talked with me saying, What are these, my lord? Then the angel that talked with me answered and said unto me, Knowest thou not what these be? And I said, No, my lord. Here we see that Zechariah did not yet understand connection between the Two Anointed Ones and would be encouraged to rebuild the second temple in which their Savior would come. God is in control. He has chosen these two to work through Joshua and Zerubbabel, during Zechariah's time in the Old Covenant as well as in the New Covenant through the two witnesses.

God's angel explains to him how the Lord is going to do this, in the next verse. NOT BY MIGHT NOR BY POWER, BUT BY MY SPIRIT, SAITH THE LORD OF HOSTS. Not by the might of man, nor by the power of the flesh, but by God's Spirit will He accomplish His Word. Just as the oil flowed without the help of man thru the lamp stand. This oil is symbolic of the Holy Spirit.

In Zechariah 4:8-9 the angel of the Lord said to Zechariah, You will see Zerubbabel begin and finish the rebuilding of my temple in your days. 4:10 For who hath despised the day of small things? For they shall rejoice, and shall see the plummet in the hand of Zerubbabel with those seven; they are the eyes of the LORD; which run to and fro through the whole earth. During their short time here on earth, many people will despise the two Anointed Ones ministry.

Also a plum line is a device used to make sure the walls are strait and true. This is symbolic of their ministry. The eyes of the LORD will make sure it is accomplished. Our wall of safety is our LORD JESUS CHRIST. The two Anointed Ones preach the TRUTH about the true Christ but infuriately many will say at the true Christ's coming, 'Lord did we not prophecy, heal and cast out demons in your name? And the Lord will say "Away, I never knew you."

Many truths have been given unto us in open visions and dreams concerning the condition of many of the church's people in this last day generation. My brother and I are not to keep these Truths to ourselves but blow the trumpet of warning to all that will listen to the LORDS words. We understand that Paul's gospel in the New Testament is the working of the antichrist spirit. And much of the true teaching of Christ has been tampered with. We are anointed, called and have been prepared to lead the children out of spiritual Babylon and prepare the way for the lord's second return. And we also realize God is preparing a mighty army of true believers who have been anointed and chosen for this very special time. To have a Bride without spot, wrinkle or blemish for Jesus Christ return.

Since my divorce the LORD has sent me a beautiful woman named Janine and we were married on the date 2-24-01. Look up Genesis 2-24. We fasted and prayed for Gods direction before we stepped out on our own. God's Holy Spirit awakened Janine all three nights during our fast at exactly 2:24 A.M. We then knew we had God's blessing. We then gave thanks to God for being faithful in answering our prayers. We then asked God to By His Spirit to come to our wedding. And at 2:24 P.M. we were pronounced man

111

and wife by a pastor in 2001. And truly all my loses and then some have been replenished.

To me giving God my whole life is the most important thing I have ever done. And I believe Janine represents the Holy Bride of Christ, because she has always been true and loving to me alone. We know God is putting together a mighty army of true believers and every part of the body is just important as any other part.

The Gospel of the Holy Twelve
Lection XC verse 4- Behold this crystal: how the one light it's manifest in twelve faces, yea four times twelve, and each face reflected one ray of light, and one regarded one face, and another, but it is the one crystal and the one light that shineth in all.

Lection LXV1-12 AGAIN Jesus taught them saying, God hath raised up witnesses to the truth in every nation and every age, that all might know the will of the Eternal and do it, and after that, enter into the kingdom, to be rulers and workers with the Eternal.

THE MEANING OF THE CRYSTALS
God is power, Love and Wisdom, and these three are One. God is Justice, Knowledge and Purity, and these three are One. God is Splendour, Compassion and Holiness, and these three are One. And these four Trinities are one in the hidden Diety, the Perfect, the Infinite, the Onely.

Likewise in every man who is perfected, there are three persons, that of the son, that of the spouse. And that of the father, and these three are one. So in every woman who is Perfected are there three persons, that of the daughter, that of the bride, and that of the mother, and these three are one; and the man and woman are one, even as God is One. Thus it is with God the Father-Mother, in Whom is neither male nor female and in Whom is both, and each is threefold, and all are One in the hidden Unity.

112

Marvel not at this, for as it is above so it is below, and as it is below so it is above, and that which is on earth is so, because it is so in Heaven. Again I say unto you, I and my Bride are one, even as Maria Magdalena, whom I have chosen and sanctified unto Myself as a type, is one with Me; and My Church are One. And the Church of the first born is the Maria of God. Thus saith the Eternal, she is My Mother and she hath ever conceived Me, and brought Me forth as Her Son in every age and clime. She is My Bride, everyone in Holy Union with Me her Spouse. She is My Daughter, for she hath ever issued and proceeded from Me her Father, rejoicing in Me. And these two Trinities are One in the Eternal, and are strewn forth in each man and woman who are made perfect, ever being born of God, ever conceiving and bringing forth God for the salvation of the many.

This is the Mystery of the Trinity in Humanity, and moreover in every individual child of man must be accomplished the mystery of God, every witnessing to light, suffering for the truth, ascending into Heaven, and sending forth the Spirit of Truth. And this is the path of salvation, for the Kingdom of God is within.

Lection XX111 Verse 7- but the water that I shall give him shall be in him a well of water springing up into everlasting life.

Lection XXV111 Verse 8- They who believe in me, out of their hearts shall flow rivers of water, and that which is given unto them shall they speak with power, and their doctrine shall be living water.

Verse 10- whosoever drinketh of the water that I shall give shall never thirst, but the water which cometh from God shall be in them a well of water, springing up unto everlasting life.

Lection XXV Verse 2- Blessed are they who hunger and thirst after righteousness: for they shall be filled.

Verse 7- ye are the light of the world.

Chapter 17

The Ones That Don't Belong

The dream began while I, Paul Maddock, was on a white sand beach that overlooked a crystal sea. To my left stood a small group of palm trees, and a foot path, headed toward the crystal sea, meandered through them. A woman there whom I knew from Church, was sitting on the white sand, about 15 feet to the right of me, and my child, along with her two children, were running down the path. Both she and I were looking at the crystal sea, and I had a feeling she too, wanted to swim in it.

I could see a reef just off shore that was the color of a rainbow, and many different kinds of fish were all around it. I knew that some of the fish did not belong there. About that time the woman from the Church came over and sat down beside me, and tried to seduce me. She even showed me one of her breasts. When that happened, I instantly jumped up and ran to retrieve my under water spear gun. And, as I returned with my weapon, I was prepared to fire upon the fish that did not belong in the crystal sea. Then the dream ended.

While the dream had been quite short, it still contained a great amount of truth and knowledge. First of all, I would like to address the palm trees and the foot path. **The palm trees is where Jesus often went and taught his beloved disciples,** as found in this Verse of the Gospel of the Holy Twelve, which is below. And, in Verse 3, Jesus states, **"He is the way,** the Truth and the Life." **The way, is the foot path** that traveled among the palm trees, where Jesus often taught His disciples, the genuine doctrine of the Kingdom.

Gospel of the Holy Twelve
The Confession of the Twelve Christ the True Rock
Lection XLIV:1-9

Verse 1. AGAIN Jesus sat near the sea, **in a circle of twelve palm trees**, where he oft resorted, and the Twelve and their fellows came unto him, and they sat under the shade of the trees, **and the holy One' taught them sitting in their midst.**

Verse 2. And Jesus said unto them, ye have heard what men in the world say concerning me, but whom do ye say that I am? Peter rose up with Andrew his brother and said, **Thou art the Christ, the Son of the living God, who descendeth from heaven and dwelleth in the hearts of them who believe and obey unto righteousness.** And the rest rose up and said, each after his own manner, **These words are true, so we believe.**

Verse 3. **And Jesus answered them saying, Blessed are ye my twelve who believe, for flesh and blood hath not revealed this unto you, but the spirit of God which dwelleth in you. I indeed am the way, the Truth and the Life; and the Truth understandeth all things.**

Verse 4. **All truth is in God, and I bear witness unto the truth.** I am the true Rock, and on this Rock do I build my Church, and the gates of Hades shall not prevail against it, and out of this Rock shall flow rivers of living water to give life to the peoples of the earth.

Verse 5. Ye are my chosen twelve. In me, the Head and Corner stone, are the twelve foundations of my house builded on the rock, **and on you in me shall my Church be built, and in truth and righteousness shall my Church be established.**

Verse 6. And ye shall sit on twelve thrones and send forth light and truth to all the twelve tribes of Israel after the Spirit, and I will be with you, even unto the end of the world.

Verse 7. **But there shall arise after you, men of perverse minds who shall through ignorance or through craft, suppress many things which I have spoken unto you, and lay to me things which I never taught, sowing tares among the good wheat which I have given you to sow in the world.**

Verse 8. Then shall the truth of God endure the contradiction of sinners, for thus it hath been, and thus it will be. **But the time cometh when the things which they have hidden shall be revealed and made known, and the truth shall make free those which were bound.**

Verse 9. One is your Master, all ye are brethren, and one is not greater than another in the place which I have given unto you, for ye have one Master, even Christ, who is over you and with you and in you, and there is no inequality among my twelve, or their fellows.

In the above scripture of Verse 7, Jesus warned his disciples that men of perverse minds through craft or through ignorance will change many things which Christ originally taught. And the time is at hand, that these things in which the tares have changed, are now beginning to be revealed. At the heart of the Tares gospel is, Vicarious Atonement, in other words, someone blameless had to die and pay the price for our sins and purchase our salvation. That is a counterfeit doctrine, and throughout this dream, the Holy Spirit has guided me to help others, to hopefully understand the difference between the two gospels.

Next in the dream, I was shown by the Holy Spirit, **a woman from the Church, who's children were running down the path with my child,** towards the crystal sea. The children in the dream were shown to be around the age of three or four years old. **These children upon the path, represent new converts,** pertaining to the two opposing doctrines, thus being their fundamental truths. Jesus makes this very clear in the following scripture below, that we should be innocent and teachable as little children.

Gospel of the Holy Twelve
Concerning Little Children
Lection LV11:1-2
Verse 1. AT the same time came the disciples unto Jesus, saying, who is the greatest in the Kingdom of Heaven? **And Jesus called a little child unto him and set him in**

117

the midst of them and said, Verily I say unto you, **except ye be converted and become innocent and teachable as little children, ye shall not enter into the Kingdom of Heaven,**
Verse 2. Whosoever therefore shall humble himself as this little child, the same is the greatest in the Kingdom of Heaven. And whoso shall receive one such little child in my name receiveth me.

The woman represents symbolically, the great whore, the Defiled Church, spoken of in the King James Bible, KJV, in the book of Revelation. (Hereinafter, quoted Bible Verses will be of the King James Bible, KJV).

The woman representing the Defiled Church, which had been Jesus' Church that He had built upon His Apostles, has been found to be unfaithful to Jesus Christ, and His teachings, because she, the Defiled Church, has loved another Christ, and embraced a corrupted, counterfeit doctrine.

REVELATION 17:1-6 & 12-18
Judgment of the Great Whore
Verse 1. AND there came one of the seven angels which had the seven vials, and talked with me, saying unto me, **Come hither; I will shew unto thee the judgment of the great whore that sitteth upon many waters:**
Verse 2. With whom the kings of the earth have committed fornication, and the inhabitants of the earth have been made drunk with the wine of her fornication. "**Her doctrine.**"
Verse 3. So he carried me away in the spirit into the wilderness: (**and I saw a woman sit upon a scarlet colored beast,**) "**The Evil One's Worldly System.**" full of names of blasphemy, having seven heads and ten horns.
Verse 4. **And the woman was arrayed** in purple and scarlet color, and decked with gold and precious stones and pearls, **having a golden cup in her hand full of abominations and filthiness of her fornication**; "Her doctrine."

118

Verse 5. And upon her forehead was a name written, MYSTERY, BABYLON THE GREAT, THE MOTHER OF HARLOTS AND ABOMINATIONS OF THE EARTH. **"The Hub of all the Defiled Churches."**

Verse 6. **And I saw the woman drunken with the blood of the saints, and with the blood of the martyrs of Jesus: and when I saw her, I wondered with great admiration.** **"Her Hatred Toward The True Worshipers Of Christ."**

Verse 12. **And the ten horns which thou sawest are ten kings,** which have received no kingdom as yet; but receive power as kings one hour with the beast.

Verse 13. **These have one mind, and shall give their power and strength unto the beast.**

Verse 14. **These shall make war with the Lamb, and the Lamb shall overcome them**: for he is Lord of lords, and King of kings: and they that are with him are called and chosen, and faithful.

Verse 15. And he saith unto me, **The waters which thou sawest, where the whore sitteth,** are peoples, and multitudes, and nations, and tongues. "The immense size and power of the defiled church."

Verse 16. **And the ten horns which thou sawest upon the beast, these shall hate the whore, and shall make her desolate and naked, and shall eat her flesh, and burn her with fire.**

Verse 17. **For God hath put in their hearts to fulfill his will**, and to agree, and give their kingdom unto the beast, until the words of God shall be fulfilled.

Verse 18. **And the woman which thou sawest is that great city,** which reigneth over the kings of the earth. **"The Vatican, her capital."**

REVELATION 18: 4-5

Verse 4. And I heard another voice from heaven, saying, **Come out of her, my people, that ye be not partakers of her sins, and that ye receive not of her plagues.**

Verse 5.For her sins have reached unto heaven, and God hath remembered her iniquities.

In the dream, the woman from the Church is **symbolically The Great Whore,** which is shown here in the Book of Revelation. She is called that, because she was not true to Christ's original teachings. She went whoring after another Christ's doctrine. Anti-Christ means, another christ. Therefore she becomes Defiled to Jesus Christ, and He will reject her, if she does not repent.

How do we know this? Because in Revelation 18:4-5 it states:

Verse 4. And I heard another voice from heaven, saying, **Come out of her my people**, that ye be not partakers of her sins, and that ye receive not of her plagues.

Verse 5. For her sins have reached unto heaven, and God hath remembered her iniquities.

Though her numbers be as the sand of the seashore, only a small remnant will remain. And, the few that make it through the great tribulation of those days, will be holy unto the Lord. But great punishment will they receive, before it ends. You don't want to be in that number. You must understand many of God's children have been deceived by the counterfeit gospel of another Christ. That counterfeit gospel was taught by Apostle Paul, and later was embraced by Roman Emperor Constantine.

Constantine was Emperor of Rome in the years of A.D. 280-337, and he converted over to the Anti-Christ version of Christianity in the year of A.D. 312, until his death. In the year of A.D. 325, Constantine had the scriptures canonized at the meeting of many priest, at Nicaea in Bithynia. Reverend Davis does a remarkable and anointed work on this subject.

Next in the dream, the woman tried to seduce me, which means, she made an attempt to persuade me to embrace her doctrine that had been taught by Apostle Paul. **She even revealed one of her breast,** as she boldly kept trying to seduce me. That has a symbolic meaning, and it is

120

explained in the scripture below. **Praise God for the Holy Spirits aid, in helping me understand and warn others.**

HEBREWS 5:9-14
Verse 9. And being made perfect, he became the author of eternal salvation unto all them that obey him;
Verse 10. Called of God an high priest after the order of Melchisedec.
Verse 11. Of whom we have many things to say, and hard to be uttered, **seeing ye are dull of hearing.**
Verse 12. **For when for the time ye ought to be teachers, ye have need that one teach you again which be the first principles of the oracles of God; and are become such as have need of milk, and not of strong meat.**
Verse 13. **For every one that useth milk is unskillful in the word of righteousness: for he is a babe.**
Verse 14. But strong meat belonged to them that are of full age, even those who by reason of use have their senses exercised to discern both good and evil.

As the woman in the dream tried to seduce me, to symbolically embrace her defiled doctrine of another Christ, she then revealed her breast to me. The symbol of her breast is found in the above portion of scripture from Hebrews 5:13. **For every one that useth milk is unskillful in the word of righteousness**: for he is a babe. **In other words, the doctrine I followed, which is the Law of Love, to her had no merit.**

In the dream, she was shown sitting upon the sand to my right. I was perplexed by this, because I understood by reading the scriptures, the righteous are always shown to be on the right side of God. **The Holy Spirit revealed to me, (it must be seen from God's point of view.)** If I was to view her from the direction of God's throne, then she would be seated towards the left side, from God's observation.

Jesus speaks about the separation between two very different groups, that are called by His name.

Gospel of the Holy Twelve
The Sheep And The Goats
Lection LXV11:7-15
Verse 7. When the Son of man shall come in his glory and all the holy angels with him, then shall he sit upon the throne of his glory. And before him shall be gathered all nations, and he shall separate them one from another, **as a shepherd divideth his sheep from the goats**. And he shall set the sheep on his right hand, **but the goats on the left**.
Verse 8. Then shall the King say unto them on his right hand, Come ye blessed of my Parent, inherit the kingdom prepared for you from the foundation of the world. For I was an hungered and ye gave me food. I was thirsty and ye gave me drink. I was a stranger and ye took me in. Naked and ye clothed me. I was sick and ye visited me. I was in prison and ye came unto me.
Verse 9. Then shall the righteous answer him, saying, Lord, when saw we thee an hungered and fed thee? Or thirsty and gave thee drink? When saw we thee a stranger and took thee in? or naked and clothed thee? Or when saw we thee sick, or in prison and came unto thee?
Verse 10. And the King shall answer and say unto them, **Behold, I manifest myself unto you, in all created forms;** and verily I say unto you, Inasmuch as ye have done it unto the least of these my brethren, ye have done it unto me.
Verse 11. **Then shall he say also unto them on his left hand, Depart from me ye evil souls into the eternal fires which ye have prepared for yourselves, till ye are purified seven times and cleansed from your sins**.
Verse 12. For I was an hungered and ye gave me no food, I was thirsty and ye gave me no drink, I was a stranger and ye took me not in, naked and ye clothed me not, sick and in prison and ye visited me not.
Verse 13. Then shall they also answer him, saying, Lord, when saw we thee an hungered, or athirst, or a stranger, or naked, or in prison, and did not minister unto thee?

Verse 14. Then shall he answer them, saying, **Behold I manifest myself unto you, in all created forms,** and Verily I say unto you, Inasmuch as ye did it not to the least of these, my brethren, ye did it not unto me.

Verse 15. **And the cruel and the loveless shall go away into chastisement** for a**ges, and if they repent not, be utterly destroyed; but the righteous and the merciful, shall go into life and peace everlasting.**

Jesus teaches in the Gospel of the Holy Twelve that we are to be loving and kind whenever possible, to our brothers and sisters. The animal kingdom is also included in His command. Jesus was given the Law of Love, from ALL MIGHTY GOD above. And our Lord Jesus came to earth to establish, and teach us His Father's most precious Law. Also when Jesus was on the Mount, during the transfiguration and the giving of The Law, **six glories** were seen upon Him by his disciples. These six glories are the colors of the rainbow, which is the sign of God's covenant.

In the dream I was shown within the clear lake, a **reef that was the color of a rainbow**. The rainbow was first mentioned back in GENESIS. It represents God's covenant between Noah and his seed, and all living creatures that there would never again be a destroying world flood, covering the whole earth.

GENESIS 9: 8-13

Covenant with Noah

Verse 8. And God spake unto Noah, and to his sons with him, saying,

Verse 9. And I, behold, I establish my covenant with you, and with your seed after you;

Verse 10. And with every living creature that is with you, of the fowl, of the cattle, and of every beast of the earth with you; from all that go out of the ark, to every beast of the earth.

Verse 11. **And I will establish my covenant with you;** neither shall all flesh be cut off any more by the waters of a flood; neither shall there any more be a flood to destroy the earth.

Verse 12. And God said, This is the token of the covenant which I make between me and you and every living creature that is with you, for perpetual generations:

Verse 13. **I do set my bow in the cloud, and it shall be for a token of a covenant between me and the earth.**

In the dream, I was shown **the reef with the colors of the rainbow upon it. These colors are the colors of God's covenant**, the same colors shown to Noah, long ago. **Also a reef provides a living habitat for all life around it,** including the fish. Here is a (PHD Physicist) on **how many colors are in the rainbow**? (PHD Physicist responds.) Red, orange, yellow, green, blue and violet. (Some people include the violet color of indigo as a separate color.) We can perceive more colors than that if we want to by slicing it up more carefully-between red and orange there's a red-orange color that can be differentiated, etc. But we usually stick with roughly **6 as the answer.**

Gospel of the Holy Twelve
The Transfiguration on the Mount The Giving of the Law
Lection XLV1:4-7
Verse 4. Then Peter said unto Jesus, Lord, it is good for us to be here; if thou wilt let us make here three tabernacles; one for thee, and one for Moses, and one for Elias.

Verse 5. While he yet spake, behold a bright cloud overshadowed them, and twelve rays as of the sun issued from behind the cloud, and a voice came out of the cloud, which said, **This is my beloved Son, In whom I am well pleased; hear ye him.**

Verse 6. And when the disciples heard it, they fell on their faces and were sore amazed, and Jesus came and touched them and said, Arise and be not afraid. And when they had lifted up their eyes, they saw no man, save Jesus only. **"And the six glories were seen upon him."**

Verse 7. **AND Jesus said unto them, Behold a new law I give unto you, which is not new but old, Even as Moses**

gave the Ten Commandments to Israel after the flesh, so also I give unto you the Twelve for the Kingdom of Israel after the Spirit.

The factual point I wanted to make here is this: the number of covenant colors are six. In Verse 5, from the previous scriptures of the Gospel of the Holy Twelve, JOVA GOD says: "This is my beloved Son, In whom I am well pleased; hear ye him. And when the disciples heard it, they fell on their faces and were sore amazed, and Jesus came and touched them and said, Arise and be not afraid. Then Verse 6 stated, "And when they had lifted up their eyes, they saw no man, save Jesus only. **And the six glories were upon him."** The disciples saw the six glorious colors of God's covenant upon Jesus, the six colors of the rainbow! Immediately after that, Jesus gave the Twelve Laws of Love.

The reef I was shown in the clear lake, represents God's covenant through Christ, and all those who love and obey His Holy Law will be saved. Then, and only then, will they be able to enjoy the abundant life of God's kingdom. **That is the meaning of the six glorious colors upon the reef**, that gives this abundant life **to the fish, who have stayed pure to Christ's genuine teachings. The fish that did not belong in the crystal sea**, were associated with **the defiled teachings of another christ**. That is why they did not belong there, even though they are called by Christ name.

My brother Russell and myself have been anointed to bring forth a message of knowledge and amendment, to the defiled Churches. Hopefully, we pray, that some will embrace the Law of Love, Jesus originally taught. Russell felt the power of the anointing, I was shown it. And, as I beheld the great wonders of the anointing, I too was shown the colors of the rainbow, within my Vessel. The reason being: the Two witnesses are the fore runners of Jesus

Christ's message to the Churches; and secondly to the whole world.

The Two Witnesses help prepare the way for the Lord of lords and King of kings; they make straight the crooked path. What has been done in darkness will be brought to the light. If the people in the Defiled Churches don't listen and repent, then they will experience the great tribulation. But those who violently appose their message, will be dealt with, and dealt with very strongly; thus the meaning of the weapon used against the fish that did not belong.

This message will thunder in the hearing of the Defiled Churches.

REVELATION 11:3-5
Verse 3. **And I will give power unto my two witnesses,** and they shall prophesy a thousand two hundred and threescore days, clothed in sackcloth. (Because they know the terrible judgment that is coming upon those who reject the Law of Love.)
Verse 4. These are the two olive trees, and the two candlesticks standing before the God of the earth.
Verse 5. **And if any man will hurt them, fire proceeded out of their mouth, and devoured their enemies:** and if any man will hurt them, he must in this manner be killed.

Again, we pray that many will repent and embrace the Law of Love Jesus originally taught.

JOHN 10:10. The thief cometh not, but for to steal, and to kill, and to destroy: **I am come that they might have life, and that they might have it more abundantly.**

First of all I am going to bring forth some scriptures from Apostle Paul's version of salvation, so we can compare it to the original teachings of Christ, taken from the Gospel of the Holy Twelve. Doing so will shed light upon that which has been done in darkness.

126

EPHESIANS 1: 5-7

THE EPISTLE OF PAUL THE APOSTLE TO THE
EPHESIANS

Verse 5. Having predestinated us unto the adoption of
children by Jesus Christ to himself, according to the good
pleasure of his will,

Verse 6. To the praise of the glory of his grace, wherin he
hath made us accepted in the beloved.

Verse 7. **In whom we have redemption through his
blood, the forgiveness of sins**, according to the riches of
his grace. **(Vicarious- Atonement)**

This is just another form of a bloody sacrifice. In other
words, someone's innocent blood takes away our sin. **This
is the canonized version that has had precedence over
the genuine gospel, which has been embraced in most of
the Churches, for such a long time.** Jesus speaks out
against that teaching in this portion of scripture below.

Gospel of the Holy Twelve

By The Shedding Of Blood Of Others Is No Remission Of
Sins

Lection XXX111:1-5

Verse 1. JESUS was teaching his disciples in the outer
court of the Temple and one of them said unto him: Master,
it is said by the priests that without shedding of blood there
is no remission. Can then the blood offering of the law take
away sin?

Verse 2. And Jesus answered: No blood offering, of beast
or bird, or man, can take away sin, **for how can the
conscience be purged from sin by the shedding of
innocent blood**? Nay, it will increase the condemnation.

Verse 3. The priests indeed receive such offering as a
reconciliation of the worshippers for the trespasses against
the law of Moses, **but for sins against the Law of God
there can be no remission, save by repentance and
amendment.**

127

Verse 4. **Is it not written in the prophets, Put your blood sacrifices to your burnt offerings, and away with them, and cease ye from the eating of flesh**, for I spake not to your fathers nor commanded them, when I brought them out of Egypt, concerning these things? But this thing I commanded saying:

Verse 5. Obey my voice and walk in the ways that I have commanded you, and ye shall be my people, and it shall be well with you. But they hearkened not, nor inclined their ear.

Christ's true believers worship the Lord in Spirit and in Truth, according to the Law of Love Jesus taught to his true followers. I know Reverend Roderick C. Davis, my Brother Russell, and myself, have written the Twelve Laws of Love a number of times in our writings, but it cannot be stressed enough, because our very salvation depends upon understanding, repenting, and following the Holy Law. I feel led, to write it here again.

Gospel of the Holy Twelve
The Transfiguration on the Mount The Giving of the Law
Lection XLV1:7-24
Verse 7. **AND Jesus said unto them, Behold a new law I give unto you, which is not new but old**. Even as Moses gave the Ten Commandments to Israel after the flesh, **so also I give unto you the Twelve for the Kingdom of Israel after the Spirit.**

Verse 8. **For who are the Israel of God? Even they of every nation and tribe who work righteousness, love mercy and keep my commandments, these are the true Israel of God**. And standing upon his feet, Jesus spake, saying:

Verse 9. **Hear O Israel, JOVA, thy God is One; many are My seers, and My prophets. In Me all live and move, and have subsistence.**

Verse 10. **Ye shall not take away the life of any creature for your pleasure, nor for your profit, nor yet torment it.**

Verse 11. Ye shall not steal the goods of any, nor gather lands and riches to yourselves, beyond your need or use.

Verse 12. **Ye shall not eat the flesh, nor drink the blood of any slaughtered creature**, no yet any thing which bringeth disorder to your health or senses.

Verse 13. Ye shall not make impure marriages, where love and health are not, nor yet corrupt yourselves, or any creature made pure by the Holy.

Verse 14. Ye shall not bear false witness against any, nor willfully deceive any by a lie to hurt them.

Verse15. Ye shall not do unto others, as ye would not that others should do unto you.

Verse 16. Ye shall worship One Eternal, the Father-Mother in Heaven, of Whom are all things, and reverence the holy Name.

Verse 17. Ye shall revere your fathers and your mothers on earth, whose care is for you, and all the teachers of Righteousness.

Verse 18. Ye shall cherish and protect the weak, and those who are oppressed, **and all creatures that suffer wrong**.

Verse 19. **Ye shall work with your hands the things that are good and seemly; so shalt ye eat the fruits Of the earth,** and live long in the land.

Verse 20. Ye shall purify yourselves daily **and rest the Seventh Day from labour**, **keeping holy the Sabbaths** and the Festival of your God.

Verse 21. Ye shall do unto others as ye would that others should do unto you.

Verse 22. And when the disciples heard these words, they smote upon their breasts saying: Wherein we have offended. O God forgive us: and may thy wisdom, love and truth within us incline our hearts to love and Keen this Holy Law.

Verse 23. And Jesus said unto them, My yoke is equal and my burden light, if ye will to bear it, to you it will be easy. **Lay no other burden on those that enter into the kingdom, but only these necessary things**.

Verse 24. This is the new Law unto the Israel of God, and the Law is within, for it is the Law of Love, **and it is not**

new but old. Take heed that ye add nothing to this law, neither take anything from it. Verily I say unto you, **they who believe and obey this law shall be saved**, [and they who know and obey it not, shall be lost].

Here Christ our Lord, gave to His disciples the Holy Law of Love. And Jesus says in Verse 24. **Take heed that ye add nothing to this law, neither take anything from it. They who believe and obey this law shall be saved, and they who know and obey it not, shall be lost.**

Below, is apostle Paul's version of two very important laws that he ignores. Number one, we are not to eat the flesh of any animal. And number two, we are to keep the Sabbath day Holy. And further down in Colossians, he even boldly proclaims that the Law, was nailed to the cross!

ROMANS 14:1-6
Judge Not Thy Brother
Verse 1. **HIM that is weak in the faith receive ye**, but not to doubtful disputations.
Verse 2. **For one believeth that he may eat all things**: another, **who is weak, eateth herbs**.
Verse 3. Let not him that eateth despise him that eateth not; and let not him which eateth not judge him that eateth: for God hath received him.
Verse 4. **Who art thou that judgest another man's servant?** To his own master he standeth or falleth. Yea, he shall be holden up: for God is able to make him stand.
Verse 5. One man esteemed one day above another: **another esteemed every day alike**. Let every man be fully persuaded in his own mind.
Verse 6. **He that regarded the day, to the Lord he doth not regard it.** He that eateth, eateth to the Lord, for he giveth God thanks; and he that eateth not, and giveth God thanks.
Verse 7. For none of us liveth to himself, and no man dieth to himself.

Verse 8. For whether we live, we live unto the Lord; and whether we die, we die unto the Lord: **whether we live therefore, or die, we are the Lord's**.

In the above portion of scripture from Verse 1, Paul clearly teaches: one who is weak receive ye, but not to doubtful disputations, **(order.)** And in Verse 2, he states: for one believth that he may eat all things; **another, who is weak, eateth herbs.** In other words, one who is not schooled properly, eats herbs. In the Gospel of the Holy Twelve Jesus condemns those who eat flesh, and wrongfully kill God's creatures. And Jesus goes on to state that those who kill God's creatures whose hands are stained with blood, and those who consume their flesh, **cannot be righteous, nor can they teach the ways, of the kingdom of God.**

Gospel of the Holy Twelve
Jesus Condemneth The Ill Treatment of Animals
Lection XXXV111:1-5
Verse 1. AND some of his disciples came and told him of a certain Egyptian, a son of Belial, who taught that it was lawful to torment animals, if their sufferings brought any profit to men.
Verse 2. And Jesus said unto them, **Verily I say unto you, they who partake of benefits which are gotten by wronging one of God's creatures, cannot be righteous**: nor can they touch holy things, or **teach the mysteries of the kingdom, whose hands are stained With blood, or whose mouths are defiled with flesh**.
Verse 3. **God giveth the grains and the fruits of the earth for food: and for righteous man truly there is no other lawful sustenance for the body.**
Verse 4. The robber who breaketh into the house made by man is guilty, **but they who break into the house made by God, even of the least of these are the greater sinners. Wherefore I say unto all who desire to be my disciples, keep your hands from bloodshed and let no flesh meat enter your mouths, for God is just and**

bountiful, who ordained that man shall live by the fruits and seeds of the earth alone.

Verse 5. But if any animal suffer greatly, and if its life be a misery unto it, or if it be dangerous to you, release it from its life quickly, and with as little pain as you can, Send it forth in love and mercy, but torment it not, and God the Father-Mother will shew mercy unto you, as ye have shown mercy unto those given into your hands.

Next Jesus addresses the Sabbath day.

Gospel of the Holy Twelve
Lection XL1:7-9
Verse 7. AND Jesus beheld a man working on the Sabbath, and he said unto him, Man, if thou knowest not the law in the spirit; but if thou knowest not, thou art accursed and a transgresor of the law.

Verse 8. **And again Jesus said unto his disciples, what shall be done unto these servants who, knowing their Lord's will, prepare not themselves for his coming, neither do according to his will**?

Verse 9. Verily I say unto you, They that know their Master's will, and do it not, shall be beaten with many stripes. **But they who not knowing their Master's will, do it not, shall be beaten with but few stripes.** To whomsoever much is given, of them is much required. And to whom little is given from them is required but little.

In this portion of scripture, **Jesus made it very clear the Sabbath is to be obeyed. Listen to apostle Paul's doctrine of another Christ**, which truly transgresses the Law of Love, that Jesus originally taught.

COLOSSIANS 2:10-23
Established in the Faith
Verse 10. **And ye are complete in him, which is the head of all principality and power:**

Verse 11. In whom also ye are circumcised with the circumcision made without hands, in putting off the body of the sins of the flesh by the circumcision of Christ:

Verse 12. Buried with him in baptism, wherin also ye are risen with him through the faith of the operation of God, who hath raised him from the dead.

Verse 13. And you, being dead in your sins and the uncircumcision of your flesh, hath he quickened together with him, **having forgiven you all trespasses**;

Verse 14. **Blotting out the handwriting of ordinances that was against us, which was contrary to us, and took it out of the way, (nailing it to his cross;)**

Verse 15. And having spoiled principalities and powers, he made a shew of them openly, triumphing over them in it.

Verse 16. **Let no man therefore judge you in meat**, or in drink, or in respect of an holyday, or of the new moon, **or of the Sabbath days**:

Verse 17. Which are a shadow of things to come; **but the body is of Christ**.

Verse 18. Let no man beguile you of your reward in a voluntary humility and worshipping of angels, intruding into those things which he hath not seen, vainly puffed up by his fleshly mind,

Verse 19. And not holding the Head, from which all the body by joints and bands having nourishment ministered, and knit together, increaseth with the increase of God.

Verse 20. **Wherefore if ye be dead with Christ from the rudiments of the world, why, as though living in the world, are ye subject to ordinances**,

Verse 21. (**Touch not; taste not; handle not;**

Verse 22. Which all are to perish with the using;) after the commandments and doctrines of men?

Verse 23. **Which things have indeed a shew of wisdom in will-worship**, and humility, and neglecting of the body; not in any honour to the satisfying of the flesh.

One must understand that there are two different doctrines of Christ. And one must agree, that apostle Paul's doctrine does not embrace the Law of Love, which Jesus originally

133

taught to His disciples. Jesus states in the Gospel of the Holy Twelve, that God gave unto man in the beginning all manner of seed, and fruit of the trees, and seed, having been for the food and healing of man and beast.

Jesus quoted from Genesis.

GENESIS 2: 29-31
Creation
Verse 29. And God said, behold, I have given you every herb bearing seed, which is upon the face of all the earth, and every tree, of all the earth, and every tree, in the which is the fruit of a tree yielding seed; to you it shall be for meat.-(**food**)
Verse 30. And to every beast of the earth, and to every fowl of the air, and to every thing that creepeth upon the earth, wherein there is life, I have given every green herb for meat: and it was so.
Verse 31. And God saw every thing that he had made, and, behold, it was very good. And the evening and the morning were the sixth day.

Here is a very important point I want to make clear from the above scriptures taken from Genesis: man was to eat a fleshless diet, and also in the beginning, the animals were to eat that way as well. This will be addressed a little further down, in the explanation of the dream.

Gospel of the Holy Twelve
The Truth Maketh Free
Lection L1:12-18
Verse 12. And certain of the Elders and Scribes from the temple came unto him saying, **Why do thy disciples teach men that it is unlawful to eat the flesh of beasts** though they be offered in sacrifice **as by Moses ordained.**
Verse 13. For it is written, God said to Noah, The fear and the dread of you shall be upon every beast of the field, and every bird of the air, and every fish of the sea, into your hand they are delivered.

Verse 14. **And Jesus said unto them, ye hypocrites**, well did Esaias speak of you, and your forefathers, sayings **This people draweth nigh unto Me, with their mouths, and honour me with their lips, but their heart is far from me, for in vain do they worship Me teaching for divine doctrines, the commandments of men in my name but to satisfy their own lusts.**

Verse 15. As also Jeremiah bear witness when he saith, concerning blood offerings and sacrifices I the Lord God commanded none of these things in the day that ye came out of Egypt, but only this I commanded you to do, righteousness, walk in the ancient paths, do justice, love mercy, and walk humbly with thy God.

Verse16. **But ye did not hearken to Me, Who in the beginning gave you all manner of seed, and fruit of the trees and seed having been for the food and healing of man and beast.** And they said, Thou speakest against the law.

Verse 17. And he said against Moses indeed I do not speak nor against the law, **but against them who corrupted his law**, which he permitted for the hardness of your hearts.

Verse 18. But, behold, a greater than Moses is here! **And they were wrath and took up stones to cast at him.** And Jesus passed through their midst and was hidden from their violence.

Jesus explained to the Elders and Scribes of the temple, who opposed the disciples of Christ, that the eating of flesh was a sin. And that the original commands of Moses, were corrupted. Also another important point I want to make: how violent and angry the Elders and Scribes became when Jesus confronted them about the genuine teachings of the Kingdom of God, that being the Law of Love.

Can one imagine how the Defiled Church is going to react when they here this message. One thing still remains: we must worship the Lord in Spirit and in Truth.

Gospel of the Holy Twelve

God the Food And Drink of All

Lection XXX11:4-9

Verse 4. For of the fruits of the trees and the seeds of the herbs alone do I partake, and these are changed by the Spirit into my flesh and my blood. Of these alone and their like shall ye eat who believe in me, and are my disciples, for of these, in the Spirit come life and health and healing unto man.

Verse 5. Verily shall my Presence be with you in the Substance and Life of God, manifested in this body, and this blood; and of these shall ye all eat and drink who believe in me.

Verse 6. For in all places I shall be lifted up for the life of the world, as it is written in the prophets; From the rising up of the sun unto the going down of the same, in every place a pure Oblation with incense shall be offered unto my Name.

Verse 7. As in the natural so in the spiritual. My doctrine and my life shall be meat and drink unto you,-the bread of Life and the Wine of Salvation.

Verse 8. **As the corn and the grapes are transmuted into flesh and blood, so must your natural minds be changed into spiritual.** Seek ye the Transmutation of the natural into Spiritual.

Verse 9. **Verily I say unto you, in the beginning, all creatures of God did find their sustenance in the herbs and the fruits of the earth alone,** till the ignorance and the selfishness of man turned many of them from the use which God had given them to that which was contrary to their original use, (**but even these shall yet return to their natural food, as it is written in the prophets, and their words shall not fail.**)

Verse 10. **Verily God ever giveth of the Eternal Life and Substance** to renew the forms of the universe. It is therefore of the flesh and blood, even the Substance and Life of the Eternal, that ye are partakers unto life, and my words are spirit and they are life.

Again, Jesus quoted from Genesis.

GENESIS 1:30. And to every beast of the earth, and to every fowl of the air, and to every thing that creepeth upon the earth, wherein there is life, I have given every green herb for meat: and it was so.

Now another amazing point needs to be understood here: Jesus also quoted the prophet Isaiah, from Verse 9, when He stated: **but even these** (carnavours,) **shall yet return to their natural food, as it is written in the prophets, and their words shall not fail.**

ISAIAH 11:1-12
Prophecy of Christ
Verse 1. AND there shall come forth a rod out of the stem of Jesse, and a branch shall grow out of his roots:
Verse 2. And the spirit of the LORD shall rest upon him, the spirit of wisdom and understanding, the spirit of counsel and might, the spirit of knowledge and of the fear of the LORD;
Verse 3. And shall make him of quick understanding in the fear of the LORD: and he shall not judge after the sight of his eyes, neither reprove after the hearing of his ears:
Verse 4. But with righteousness shall he judge the poor, and reprove with equity for the meek of the earth: **and he shall smite the earth with the rod of his mouth, and with the breath of his lips shall he slay the wicked.**
Verse 5. And righteousness shall be the girdle of his loins, and faithfulness the girdle of his reins.
Verse 6. The wolf also shall dwell with the lamb, and the leopard shall lie down with the kid; and the calf and the young lion and the fatling together; and a little child shall lead them.
Verse 7. And the cow and the bear shall feed; their young ones shall lie down together: **and the lion shall eat straw like the ox.**
Verse 8. And the sucking child shall play on the hole of the asp, and the weaned child shall put his hand on the cockatrice's den.

Verse 9. **They shall not hurt nor destroy in all my holy mountain: for the earth shall be full of the knowledge of the LORD, as the waters cover the sea.**
Verse 10 **And in that day there shall be a root of Jesse, which shall stand for an ensign of the people;** to it shall the Gentiles seek: and his rest shall be glorious. (The Elect of God.)
Verse 11. **And it shall come to pass in that day, that the Lord shall set his hand again the second time to recover the remnant of his people,** which shall be left, from Assyria, and from Egypt, and from Pathros, and from Cush, and from Elam, and from Shinar, and from Hamath, and from the islands of the sea.
Verse 12. And he shall set up an ensign for the nations, and shall assemble the outcasts of Israel, and gather together the dispersed of Judah from the four corners of the earth.

As Isaiah was given these prophetic words by the Holy Spirit, even the animals will live in harmony with each other again, like it was in the beginning, back in Genesis. This happens only when Jesus returns to earth, from the Heavens, and sets up His Kingdom here. Then all things will be restored back to their original root. That means, Thy Kingdom Come, Thy Will Be Done, On Earth, as it is in Heaven. Those words were spoken by Jesus, as He was asked by His disciples, how are we to pray.

Gospel of the Holy Twelve
Jesus Teaches How to Pray
Lection X1X:3-4
Verse 3. Our Father-Mother Who art above and within: Hallowed be Thy Name in twofold trinity. In Wisdom, Love and Equity **Thy Kingdom come to all. Thy will be done, As in Heaven so in Earth.** Give us day by day to partake of Thy holy Bread, and the fruit of the living Vine. As thou dost forgive us our trespasses, so may we forgive others who trespass against us, Shew upon us Thy goodness, that to others we may shew the same. In the hour of temptation, deliver us from evil.

Verse 4. For Thine are the Kingdom, the Power and the Glory; From the Ages of ages, Now and to the Ages of ages. Amun.

LUKE 11: 2-4
The Lord's Prayer
Verse 2. And he said unto them, When ye pray, say, Our Father which art in heaven, Hallowed be thy name. **Thy kingdom come. Thy will be done, as in heaven, so in earth.**
Verse 3. Give is day by day our daily bread.
Verse 4. And forgive us our sins; for we also forgive every one that is indebted to us. And lead us not into temptation; but deliver us from evil.

People of the Christian Churches, do you really understand the True teachings of the Kingdom of God, through Apostle Paul's version? Does it line up with the prophets words given to him by the Holy Spirit? We are given free will by God, to choose right from wrong. Do you think Jesus will accept a bride that does not honor Him, by not obeying His commands? Do you think Jesus will change your heart and mind, to align you to the Law of Love, against your will?

If we understand in the beginning, how it was before the fall of mankind, and the way it is going to be when Christ sets up His Kingdom upon earth, when all things of the Evil One will be put under our Lord's feet, then will we live in a fallen and defiled state? Apostle Paul clearly stated that the Law was to be abolished, and put on the cross. Jesus states a very different story.

MATTHEW 5: 17-18
The Sermon on the Mount
Verse 17. Think not that I am come to destroy the law, or the prophets: I am not come to destroy but to fulfill.
Verse 18. For verily I say unto you, Till heaven and earth pass, one jot or one tittle shall in no wise pass from the law, till all be fulfilled.

This is the original Christ talking here, on which were shown the six glorious colors of God's covenant. This is the Christ I hope and pray you will begin to believe!

REVELATION 4:1-6
Vision of God's Throne
Verse 1. AFTER this I looked, and, behold, a door was opened in heaven: and the first voice which I heard was as it were of a trumpet talking with me; which said, Come up hither, and I will shew thee things which must be hereafter.
Verse 2. And immediately I was in the spirit; and, behold, a throne was set in heaven, and one sat on the throne.
Verse 3. And he that sat was to look upon like a jasper and a sardine stone: **and there was a rainbow round about the throne**, in sight like unto an emerald.
Verse 4. And round about the throne were four and twenty seats: and upon the seats I saw four and twenty elders sitting, clothed in white raiment; and they had on their heads crowns of gold.
Verse 5. And out of the throne proceeded lightnings and thundering and voices: and there were seven lamps of fire burning before the throne, which are the seven Spirits of God.
Verse 6. **And before the throne there was a sea of glass like unto crystal**:

REVELATION 15:2-4
A Sea of Glass
Verse 2. **And I saw as it were a sea of glass mingled with fire:** and them that had gotten the victory over the beast, and over his image, and over his mark, and over the number of his name, **stand on the sea of glass,** having the harps of God.
Verse 3. And they sing the song of Moses the servant of God, and the song of the Lamb, saying, Great and marvelous are thy works, Lord God Almighty; just and true are thy ways, thou King of saints.

Verse 4. Who shall not fear thee, O Lord, and glorify thy name? for thou only art holy: for all nations shall come and worship before thee; for thy judgments are made manifest.

The symbol of the crystal sea represents those who have gotten the victory over the Anti Christ, and his lies through a counterfeit doctrine, even though some had to go through great tribulation because of their stubbornness. In the coming end of the current church age, God will warn souls of the Earth through His Elect, and the Two Witnesses. In the book of Revelation comes the opening of the little book of seven thunders. John sees in the vision that he is allowed to take it and prophesy at the appointed time.

REVELATION 10:1-11
The powerful angel who brought the book of seven thunders
Verse 1. AND I saw another mighty angel come down from heaven, clothed with a cloud: **and a rainbow was upon his head**, and his face was as it were the sun, and his feet as pillars of fire.
Verse 2. And he had in his hand a little book open: and he set his right foot upon the sea, and his left foot on the earth,
Verse 3. And cried with a loud voice, as when a lion roareth: and when he had cried, **seven thunders uttered their voices**.
Verse 4. And when the seven thunders had uttered their voices, I was about to write: and I heard a voice from heaven saying unto me, **Seal up those things which the seven thunders uttered, and write them not.**
Verse 5. And the angel which I saw stand upon the sea and upon the earth lifted up his hand to heaven,
Verse 6. And sware by him that liveth for ever and ever, who created heaven, and the things that therein are, and the earth, and the sea, and the things which are therein, that there should be time no longer:
Verse 7. But in the days of the voice of the seventh angel, when he shall begin to sound, **the mystery of God should**

be finished, as he hath declared to his servants the prophets.

Verse 8. **And the voice which I heard from heaven spake unto me again, and said, Go and take the little book which is open in the hand of the angel which standeth upon the sea and upon the earth.**

Verse 9. And I, (**John**) went unto the angel, and said unto him, **Give me the little book. And he said unto me, Take it,** and eat it up; and it shall make thy belly bitter, but it shall be in thy mouth sweet as honey.

Verse 10. And I took the little book out of the angel's hand, and ate it up; and it was in my mouth sweet as honey: and as soon as I had eaten it, my belly was bitter.

Verse 11. And he said unto me, **Thou must prophesy again before many peoples, and nations, and tongues, and kings.**

REVELATION 11:1, **John** is told to measure the temple of God and the altar, and those that worship therein. And in Verse 3. From the same chapter, God says, **I will give power unto my two witnesses, and they shall prophesy a thousand two hundred and threescore days, clothed in sackcloth.**

If one understands that John was told he would prophesy again before many peoples, and nations, and tongues, and kings, how could he accomplish this great and monumental task? How could he, when he was held captive as a prisoner on the Island of Patmos, because of the word of God, and the testimony of Jesus Christ? And why was John told to seal up those things which the seven thunders uttered in the little book, and write them not?

In Revelation 10:4, because this prophesy was to be given in the last days of the Church age, way into the future. And John, as being one of the Elect of God, could only accomplish this by reincarnating at a much later time. Jesus taught **reincarnation of the soul,** and **the understanding of the Elect**, in the Gospel of the Holy Twelve.

142

Gospel of the Holy Twelve
The Regeneration of The Soul
Lection XXXV11:6-8
Verse 6. The light shineth from the East even unto the West; out of the darkness, the Sun ariseth and goeth down into darkness again; so is it with man, from the ages unto the ages.
Verse 7. **When it cometh from the darkness, it is that he hath lived before, and when it goeth down again into darkness, it is that he may rest for a little, and thereafter again exist.**
Verse 8. So through many changes must ye be made perfect, as it is written in the book of Job, I am a wanderer, changing place after place and house after house, until I come unto the City and Mansion which is eternal.

Gospel of the Holy Twelve
Jesus Teacheth In The Palm Circle The Divine Life And Substance
Lection LX1V:7-13
Verse 7. From the Eternal they flow, to the Eternal they return. The spirit to Spirit, soul to Soul, mind to Mind, sense to Sense, life to Life, form to Form, dust to Dust.
Verse 8. **In the beginning God willed and there came forth the beloved Son**, the divine Love, and **the beloved Daughter**, the holy wisdom, **equally proceeding from the One Eternal Fount; and of these are the generations of the Spirits of God, the Sons and Daughters of the Eternal.**
Verse 9. **And These,** (The Elect) **descend to earth, and dwell with men and teach them the ways of God, to love the laws of the Eternal, and obey them, that in them they may find salvation.**
Verse 10. **Many nations have seen their day. Under divers names have they been revealed to them, and they have rejoiced in their light; and even now they come again unto you, but Israel receiveth them not.**

Verse 11. Verily I say unto you, my twelve whom I have chosen, that which hath been taught by them of old time is true--**though corrupted by the foolish imaginations of men**.

Verse 12. Again, Jesus spake unto Mary Magdalene saying, It is written in the law, Whoso leaveth father or mother, let him die the death. Now the law speaketh not of the parents in this life, but of the Indweller of light which is in us unto this day.

Verse 13. **Whoso therefore forsaketh Christ the Saviour, the Holy law, and the body of the Elect**, let them die the death. Yea, let them be lost in the outer darkness, for so they willed and non can hinder.

The Elect of God have reincarnated before, and taught the Law of Love to the sons and daughters of men, in past generations. They are trusted souls of Christ, and the Eternal. And, in this present day generation, just before our Lord Jesus returns for His Holy Bride, as the True Church, the Elect are here again, to aid in teaching the Law of Love to the sons and daughters of men, who are in bondage and darkness, because of the counterfeit gospel of a false Christ.

The Elect, are a mighty army of God, who will bring forth the True Gospel of the Kingdom, once again, in this last day generation of the Church age. And, they will aid in the helping of preaching the True Gospel of Jesus Christ, to bring together a glorious Church. This will be the Holy Bride of Christ that our Lord will come for.

Now more explanation on the fish in the crystal sea: to do this, one must understand the ancient symbol of the fish used in early Christian times. The fish was a secret symbol displayed on doors, or places of meetings. That came about due to the fact that back in those days, there had been great persecution toward the early followers of Christ, who were His true believers. The word ichthys, means fish in Greek, but the letters are also the initials of five greek words that mean: "Jesus Christ, Son of God, Savior" (Iesous Christos Theou Yios Soter).

Jesus told His disciples in Matthew 4:19: **"Follow Me, and I will make you fishers of men."** As the early Christians followed Christ's commands to follow and obey the Law of Love, in like manner, they were to lead others to the Lord. **The fish symbol became a natural extension of Christ's True teachings,** and also a way to recognize and identify others who knew the symbols meaning.

In the dream, the fish were swimming in the crystal sea, but I knew that some of them did not belong there. One must remember the crystal sea represents those who overcame the world, by obeying the genuine teachings of our precious Lord's doctrine. Remember what the crystal sea represents: a multitude of pure believers, around the Throne of God.

Gospel of the Holy Twelve
Lection XX:9-10
Verse 9. And I say unto you, Though ye be gathered together in my bosom, if ye keep not my commandments I will cast you forth. For if ye keep not the lesser mysteries, who shall give you the greater.
Verse 10. He that is faithful in that which is least is faithful also in much: and he that is unjust in the least is unjust also in much.

Jesus taught us God's Law of Love, which He brought from Heaven, for us to understand the commands of ALL MIGHTY GOD, and then repent and obey. This is the only way in which we can be seen worthy to obtain the Kingdom. This is the promise of God's covenant to us through His Son. I want to make this point crystal clear, in the hope that some eyes and ears will be opened to the Truth.

JOHN 3:16
Necessity of regeneration

Verse 16. For God so loved the world that he gave his only begotten Son, that whosoever believeth in him (His genuine teachings) should not perish, but have everlasting life.

1 PETER 4:17 For the time is come that judgment must begin at the house of God: and if it first begin at us, what shall the end be of them that obey not the gospel of God?

The time is coming soon when this message of the Kingdom will be spoken in their hearing, face to face, in the Churches. It will stir up many different emotions, especially when it comes to the eating of flesh, and their hunting and fishing. This will offend all the businesses that are associated with these evil atrocities. But, they will have no excuse because it will be told to them before hand.

AMOS 3:7
Warnings
Verse 7. Surely the Lord God will do nothing, but he revealed his secret unto his servants the prophets.

Gospel of the Holy Twelve
Jesus Foretelleth The End
Lection LX1:3-5
Verse 3. And in those days those that have power shall gather to themselves the lands and riches of the earth for their own lusts, and shall oppress the many who lack and hold them in bondage, and use them to increase their riches, **and they shall oppress even the beasts of the field, setting up the abominable thing. "We have the meats." But God shall send them his messenger and they shall proclaim his laws, which men have hidden by their traditions, and those that transgress shall die.**
Verse 4. Then shall they deliver you up to be afflicted, and shall kill you; and ye shall be hated of all nations for my Name's sake. And then shall many be offended, and shall betray one another, and shall hate one another. And many false prophets shall rise, and shall deceive many.

146

Verse 5. And because iniquity shall abound, the love of many shall wax cold. But he that shall endure unto the end, the same shall be saved. **And this gospel of the kingdom shall be preached in all the world for a witness unto all nations; and then shall the end come.**

There will be no excuses because the whole world is going to, once again, see and hear the True Gospel of Christ, and it shall be before the end of the Church age. It is beginning, and if you come out of the Defiled Churches, your metal will be tested. There is going to be a gathering together of the True believers of Jesus Christ's Doctrine. And, they will make up a Glorious Church that will be called the Holy Bride of Christ. I hope and pray many will be in that number.

Gospel of the Holy Twelve
The True Church
Lection LXX:10-14
Verse 10. And in their days I Jesus shall be crucified afresh and put to open shame, for they will profess to do these things in my Name. And Peter said, Be it far from thee Lord.
Verse 11. And Jesus answered, As I shall be nailed to the cross, so also shall my Church in those days, for she is my Bride and one with me. But the day shall come when this darkness shall pass away, and true Light shall shine.
Verse 12. And one shall sit on my throne, who shall be a Man of Truth and Goodness and Power, and he shall be filled with love and wisdom beyond all others, and shall rule my Church by a fourfold twelve and by two and seventy as of old, and that only which is true shall he teach.
Verse 13. And my Church shall be filled with Light, and give Light unto all nations of the earth, and there shall be one Pontiff sitting on his throne as a King and a Priest.
Verse 14. And my Spirit shall be upon him and his throne shall endure and equity, and light shall come to it, and go forth from it, to all the nations of the earth, and the Truth shall make them free. Amen.

Chapter 18

Warning: Punishment and Desolation

Holy Spirit gave me, Paul Maddock, this dream during the early morning hours of July 27, 1998, and it began as I was shown a fruit tree off in the distance, and the fruit on the tree gave off a sound similar to that which a helicopter makes when flying over your head. As I looked closer at the tree I could see what seemed to be many strange creatures on the branches, about the size of a large dragonfly.

As I walked closer, I noticed the tree was bowed from the weight of these insect like creatures. Then, suddenly, one of the creatures broke away from the tree and chased down an insect, stung it as soon as he captured it, and then promptly consumed it before flying back toward the fruit tree. As the creature was flying back to the tree, I knocked it down with my hand, right out of the air. I wanted to catch it, so I could get a good look at it, but I was uneasy, because the creature made it clear to me it could sting.

So I ran to get a pair of heavy work gloves to protect my hands, and as soon as I returned to the fruit tree, I knocked one of the creatures to the ground, and quickly snatched it with my left-gloved hand. The small creature's strength surprised me, and it slipped my grip and broke free. The creature immediately headed back up toward the fruit tree, to be with the rest of its kind, but I persisted and knocked it down again, this time catching it with both hands; I wanted time to examine it.

One thing is for sure, I had never seen such a creature in all of my days upon this earth. I will try to describe to the best of my ability, what these creatures looked like. Their face is round with black eyes that blinked. It had long gold hair from its forehead and halfway down its back. The hair was mounded up high, like a lion's mane. It had a mouth and teeth similar to that of a cat, and the whole time I was holding it, it growled and snarled at me. Its body was shaped like a huge horse fly. And its wing structure was similar to that of a horsefly, but the creature's wings were by comparison, larger in size to its body.

This creature had a large brownish-red shell around its chest and back area, which made its middle body somewhat thicker. The creatures long gold hair covered most of the shell on its back. As I held onto this powerful strange creature, I could see the huge stinger in its tail area. But at no time did the creature ever try to sting or bite me. But I must say, the thick work gloves gave me much comfort at the time. I released the strange creature and it flew back up into the tree, along with all the others, and that is when the dream ended.

The Holy Spirit urged my brother Russell to look up the word Beelzebub in his concordance, which he did, and what great meaning was shown to this dream. I thank God for my brothers obedience to our Lords will. For God has chosen us to bring a message of great importance to the Churches and the world.

THE NEW STRONGS CONCORDACE EXHAUSTIVE CONCORDANCE OF THE BIBLE *Beelzebub, Greek, 954. Beelzeboul, beh-el-zeb-ool; of Chald, or. (By parody on 1176); dung-god; Beelzebul, a name of Satan:-- Beelzubub. Baalzebuwb, Hebrew, 1176. Bah-alzeb-oob; from 1168 and 1070; Baal of (the fly; Baal-zebub, a special deity of the Ekronites: - Baalzebub. Baal, bah-al; 1168. The same as 1167 Baal, a Phoenician deity: Baal, (plur.) Baalim. Zebuwb, zeb-oob, Hebrew, 2070. From an unused root, (mean, to flit); a fly (esp. one of a sting nature):*

Bare this in mind the ancient word Beelzebub ties together Satan and these evil creatures. And shortly we will understand that these evil creatures will come forth from the bottomless pit to torment men who have not the mark of

God in their forehead in our generation. My brother and I are in our early sixties now. More on this as we proceed into the message.

The Fruit Tree symbolically represents the nation, Israel, as the Fig Tree. And one thing for sure, is that there was no fruit shown on this tree. Let the reader understand, these evil demonic creatures were on such a **fruitless** tree!

The nation of Israel at the time of Christ's Ministry was given a great national privilege to hear the genuine gospel of Christ. But for the most part, they rejected Christ's True teachings. Beginning with Abraham, and throughout their many generations, the Israelites were given much knowledge of the Messiah's coming. And, even with all this foreknowledge, they did not believe Him when He taught them in person. Why? Because the traditions of men brought forth by demons, distorted their understanding of God's Word.

Jesus' Messianic Ministry to the nation of Israel lasted three and one half years, and during that time priests, Pharisees and scribes incited many to revile Him, always looking for a way to kill Him. And Jesus knew that those who reviled the doctrine He taught, the Law of Love, that eliminated the blood sacrifice traditions of men, would do all they could to wash His Doctrine away, and He foretold such as is shown in His Gospel written by Apostle John:

Lection 44:7-8
7. But there shall arise after you, men of perverse minds who shall through ignorance or through craft, suppress many things which I have spoken unto you, and lay to me things which I never taught, sowing tares among the good wheat which I have given you to sow in the world.
8. Then shall the truth of God endure the contradiction of sinners, for thus it hath been, and thus it will be. But the time cometh when the things which they have hidden shall

be revealed and made known, and the truth shall make free those which were bound.

The two witnesses as the forerunners of Christ, and the elect of God, just before His second coming, will minister the Law of Love, which Jesus originally taught, to the defiled Churches first, and secondly to the whole world. More on this shortly.

GOSPEL OF THE HOLY TWELVE
Lection XLVI:7-9
The Transfiguration on the Mount The Giving of the Law
Verse 7. AND Jesus said unto them, Behold a new law I give unto you, which is not new but old. Even as Moses gave the Ten Commandments to Israel after the flesh, so also I give unto you the Twelve **[for the Kingdom of Israel after the Spirit.]**
Verse 8. **[For who are the Israel of God? Even they of every nation and tribe who work righteousness, love mercy and keep my commandments, these are the true Israel of God].** And standing upon his feet, Jesus spake, saying:
Verse 9. Hear O Israel, JOVA, thy God is One; many are My seers, and My prophets. In Me all live and move, and have subsistence.

This same Law of Love, that Israel rejected as a nation, will be presented again in our generation. Jesus explained to His disciples at the Transfiguration on the Mount, who the Spiritual Israel would be. It would be His chosen ones who work righteousness, love mercy, and keep His commandments. Jesus said these are the True Israel of God. Most of the Christian Churches today are defiled, because they keep not the precious Law of Love that Jesus originally taught.

GOSPEL OF THE HOLY TWELVE
Lection XLVI:10-25
The Giving of the Law

Verse 10. Ye shall not take away the life of any creature for your pleasure, nor for your profit, nor yet torment it.

Verse 11. Ye shall not steal the goods of any, nor gather lands and riches to yourselves, beyond your need or use.

Verse 12. Ye shall not eat the flesh, nor drink the blood of any slaughtered creature, nor yet any thing which bringeth disorder to your health or senses.

Verse 13. Ye shall not make impure marriages, where love and health are not, nor yet corrupt yourselves, or any creature made pure by the Holy.

Verse 14. Ye shall not bear false witness against any, nor willfully deceive any by a lie to hurt them.

Verse 15. Ye shall not do unto others, as ye would that others should do unto you.

Verse 16. Ye shall worship One Eternal, the Father-Mother in Heaven, of Whom are all things, and reverence the holy Name.

Verse 17. Ye shall revere your fathers and your mothers on earth, whose care is for you, and all the Teachers of Righteousness.

Verse 18. Ye shall cherish and protect the weak, and those who are oppressed, and all creatures that suffer wrong.

Verse 19. Ye shall work with your hands the things that are good and seemly; so shalt ye eat the fruits Of the earth, and live long in the land.

Verse 20. Ye shall purify yourselves daily and rest the Seventh Day from labour, keeping holy the Sabbaths and the Festival of your God.

Verse 21. Ye shall do unto others as ye would that others should do unto you.

Because the Israelites did not follow Gods Law, they suffered greatly. When the cup of their iniquity was full, their place of worship, **the first temple**, city and nation, was left unto them desolate. God sent unto them prophets before this great and dreadful day came upon them, in the hope that they would amend their ways and repent. But because they hardened their hearts towards God's true prophets, God rose up a powerful army to punish the

Israelites. [In the past the Israelites place of worship, the temple, was destroyed twice.] **And in our generation of the Church age, it is going to happen again, but this time to the defiled Church.** Why? Because the children of God have again gone away from Gods Law of Love.

But before this happens again, Christ is going to send His Two Witnesses and His Elect, to bring a message of repentance and amendment to the Defiled Churches, just like in the past, to the people that are called by His name. The message of the Kingdom will be preached before the great and dreadful day comes. This window period will be brief, similar to Christ's Ministry to the nation Israel.

These three different time periods are called **The Abomination of Desolation.** Let us go back in Daniel's time shortly after the destruction of Jerusalem, and the destruction of the first temple. I want to prove a very important point that Daniel, and his three friends, knew and kept, Gods Law of Love back in their time. And even during their nation's captivity, God saw them as greatly beloved. Why? Because they would not compromise God's precious Law of Love.

I am going to copy the whole chapter, because it tells of it so wonderfully. You will not hear this explanation of Gods Genuine Word behind the pulpits of the Defiled Churches today, but they will be hearing it in the very near future.

DANIEL 1:1-21, King James Bible, KJV. (hereinafter Bible Verses will be of said Bible)
Verse 1. IN the third year of the reign of Jehoiakim king of Judah **came Nebuchadnezzar king of Babylon unto Jerusalem, and besieged it.**
Verse 2. And the Lord gave Jehoiakim king of Judah into his hand, with part of the vessels of the house of God: which he carried into the land of Shinar to the house of his god; and he brought the vessels into the treasure house of his god.

Verse 3. And the king spake unto Ashpenaz the master of his eunuchs, that he should bring certain of the children of Israel, and of the king's seed, and of the princes;

Verse 4. Children in whom was no blemish, but well favored, and skilful in all wisdom, and cunning in knowledge, and understanding science, and such as had ability in them to stand in the king's palace, and whom they might teach the learning and the tongue of the Chaldeans.

Verse 5. **And the king appointed them a daily provision of the king's meat, and of the wine which he drank:** so nourishing them three years, that at the end thereof they might stand before the king.

Verse 6. Now among these were of the children of Judah, **Daniel, Hananiah, Mishael, and Azariah:**

Verse 7. Unto whom the prince of the eunuchs gave names: for he gave unto Daniel the name of Belteshazzar; and to Hananiah, of Shadrach; and to Mishael, of Meshach; and to Azariah, of Abednego.

Verse 8. **But Daniel purposed in his heart that he would not defile himself with the portion of the king's meat, nor with the wine which he drank.** [therefore he requested of the prince of the eunuchs that he might not defile himself.]

Verse 9. Now God had brought Daniel into favour and tender love with the prince of the eunuchs.

Verse 10. And the prince of the eunuchs said unto Daniel, I fear my lord the king, who hath appointed your meat and your drink: for why should he see your faces worse liking than the children which are of your sort? Then shall ye make me endanger my head to the king.

Verse 11. Then said Daniel to Jelzar whom the prince of the eunuchs had set over Daniel, Hananiah, Mishael, and Azariah,

Verse 12. Prove thy servants, I beseech thee, ten days; **and let them give us pulse to eat, and water to drink.** *(Pulse means: a plant based diet.)*

Verse 13. Then let our countenances be looked upon before thee, and the countenance of the children that eat of the portion of the king's meat: and as thou seest, deal with thy servants.

Verse 14. So he consented to them in this matter, and proved them ten days.

Verse 15. And at the end of ten days their countenances appeared fairer and fatter in flesh than all the children which did eat the portion of the king's meat.

Verse 16. **Thus Melzar took away the portion of their meat, and the wine that they should drink; and gave them pulse.**

Verse 17. **As for these four children, God gave them knowledge and skill in all learning and wisdom: and Daniel had understanding in all visions and dreams.**

Verse 18. Now at the end of the days that the king had said he should bring them in, then the prince of the eunuchs brought them in before Nebuchadnezzar.

Verse 19. And the king communed with them; **and among them all was found none like Daniel, Hananiah, Mishael, and Azariah:**

Verse 20. And in all matters of wisdom and understanding, that the king inquired of them, he found them ten times better than all the magicians and astrologers that were in all his realm.

Verse 21. And Daniel continued even unto the first year of king Cyrus.

Explanation of Pulse: The New Strong's Exhaustive Concordance of Bible explains the word **pulse**. 2235. **zeroa'**, *zay-ro-ah;* or **zeroa on,** *zay-raw-ohn'*; from 2232; something *sown* (only in the plour.), i.e. a *vegetable* (as food):--pulse.

So we read that Daniel and his three friends would not defile themselves with the eating of flesh and strong drink. And they would not compromise God's Law of Love, no matter what the outcome.

Now listen to what Apostle Paul has to say about this very important matter. Please read the whole chapter.

ROMANS 14:2 & 5-6

Judge Not Thy Brother

Verse 2. For one believeth that he may eat all things: **another, who is weak, eateth herbs.**

That is completely at odds with what Daniel and his three Israelite friends knew and obeyed; that being God's Law of Love. And in the same chapter, Paul teaches that keeping the Sabbath Day, or not keeping it at all, is of little importance.

Verse 5. One man esteemed one day above another: another esteemed every day alike. Let every man be fully persuaded in his own mind.

Verse 6. He that regarded the day, regarded it unto the Lord; and he that regarded not the day, to the Lord he doth not regard it. He that eateth, eateth to the Lord, for he giveth God thanks and he that eateth not, to the Lord he eateth not, and giveth God thanks.

Now let's hear from another Prophet who had been around, just before the time of the desolation of the first Temple. His name was Jeremiah. I am going to quote the writings from The Gospel of the Holy Twelve, because I think it is easier to understand. But I will give The Bible references pertaining to the same topic as well, that is in the Bible.

In the Gospel of The Holy Twelve, Jesus quoted Jeremiah, and explained the prophecy at the second temple to His disciples. Again, the children of Israel, even during Jesus' time, were transgressing the Law of Love. More on this topic shortly.

Gospel of the Holy Twelve
Lection XXXIII:1-10
By the Shedding Of Blood Of Others Is No Remission Of Sins

156

Verse 1. JESUS was teaching his disciples in the outer court of the Temple and one of them said unto him: Master, it is said by the priests that without shedding of blood there is no remission. Can then the blood offering of the law take away sin?

Verse 2. And Jesus answered: **No blood offering, of beast or bird, or man, can take away sin, for how can the conscience be purged from sin by the shedding of innocent blood? Nay, it will increase the condemnation.**

Verse 3. The priests indeed receive such offering as a reconciliation of the worshippers **for the trespasses against the law of Moses**, [but for sins against the Law of God there can be no remission, save by repentance and amendment.]

Verse 4. **Is it not written in the prophets, Put your blood sacrifices to your burnt offerings, and away with them, and cease ye from the eating of flesh,** for I spake not to your fathers nor commanded them, when I brought them out of Egypt, concerning these things? **But this thing I commanded saying:**

Verse 5. **Obey my voice and walk in the ways that I have commanded you, and ye shall be my people, and it shall be well with you. But they hearkened not, nor inclined their ear.**

Verse 6. And what doth the Eternal command you but to do justice, love mercy and walk humbly with your God? **Is it not written that in the beginning God ordained the fruits of the trees and the seeds and the herbs to be food for all flesh?**

Verse 7. But they have made the House of Prayer a den of thieves, and for the pure Oblation with Incense, **they have polluted my altars with blood, and eaten of the flesh of the slain.**

Verse 8. **But I say unto you: Shed no innocent blood nor eat ye flesh. Walk uprightly, love mercy, and do justly, and your days shall be long in the land.**

Verse 9. The corn that growth from the earth with the other grain, is it not transmuted by the Spirit into my flesh? The grapes of the vineyard, with the other fruits are they not

transmuted by the Spirit into my blood? [Let these, with your bodies and souls be your Memorial to the Eternal.]
Verse 10. **In these is the presence of God manifest as the Substance and as the Life of the world. Of these shall ye eat and drink for the remission of sins, and for eternal life, to all who obey my words.**

This is the reference below, where Jesus quoted Jeremiah's prophetic words to His disciples. I am not going to write them, but you can look them up in your own Bible if you like.

JEREMIAH 7:21-28
Obey My voice
Jeremiah was called to be a prophet, even before he was born in his mothers womb. He was sent with a message of warning to the children of Israel, because they had continually transgressed the Lord's Law of Love. And if they did not amend their ways and repent, and turn back to the Lord their God, then they would reap the whirlwind, meaning the Storm of the Lord upon their nation, their Holy City Jerusalem, and their Holy Temple. All would be turned into desolation. Unfortunately, because of the hardness of their hearts, that day came upon the Israelites.

JEREMIAH 1:4-10
God's Message
Verse 4. **Then the word of the LORD came unto me, saying,**
Verse 5. **Before I formed thee in the belly, I knew thee; and before thou camest forth out of the womb I sanctified thee, and I ordained thee a prophet unto the nations.**
Verse 6. Then said I, Ah, Lord GOD! Behold, I cannot speak: for I am a child.
Verse 7. But the LORD said unto me, Say not, I am a child: for thou shalt go to all that I shall send thee, and whatsoever I command thee thou shalt speak.

Verse 8. Be not afraid of their faces: for I am with thee to deliver thee, saith the LORD.

Verse 9. **Then the LORD put forth his hand, and touched my mouth. And the LORD said unto me, Behold, I have put my words in thy mouth.**

Verse 10. See, I have this day set thee over the nations and over the kingdoms, to root out, and to pull down, and to destroy, and to throw down, to build, and to plant.

JEREMIAH 24:1-10
The Figs

Verse 1. THE Lord shewed me, and, were set before the temple of the LORD, after that Nebuchadrezzar king of Babylon had carried away captive Jeconiah the son of Jehoiakim king of Judah, and the princes of Judah, with the carpenters and smiths, from Jerusalem, and had brought them to Babylon.

Verse 2. [One basket had very good figs], even like the figs that are first ripe: [and the other basket had very naughty figs], which could not be eaten, they were so bad.

Verse 3. Then said the LORD unto me, What seest thou, Jeremiah? And I said, figs; the good figs, very good; and the evil, very evil, that cannot be eaten, they are so evil.

Verse 4. Again the word of the LORD came unto me, saying,

Verse 5. **Thus saith the LORD, the God of Israel; Like these good figs, so will I acknowledge them that are carried away captive of Judah, whom I have sent out of this place into the land of the Chaldeans for their good.**

Verse 6. For I will set mine eyes upon them for good, and I will bring them again to this land: and I will build them, and not pull them down; and I will plant them, and not pluck them up.

Verse 7. And I will give them an heart to know me, that I am the LORD: and they shall be my people, and I will be their God: for they shall return unto me with their whole heart.

Verse 8. And as the evil figs, which cannot be eaten, they are so evil; surely thus saith the LORD, So will I give

Zedekiah the king of Judah, and his princes, and the residue of Jerusalem, that remain in this land, and them that dwell in the land of Egypt:

Verse 9. And I will deliver them to be removed into all the kingdoms of the earth for their hurt, to be a reproach and a proverb, a taunt and a curse, in all places whither I shall drive them.

Verse 10. And I will send the sword, the famine, and the pestilence, among them, till they be consumed from off the land that I gave unto them and to their fathers.

Here the figs symbolically represents Israel. There were some of the Israelites that still followed the Law of Love, before the desolation, and during the captivity of their land. Daniel, Hananiah, Mishael, and Azariah, are a written proven fact to this point in the Bible. Because of that which Jeremiah spoke in his day, he was hated by most of the Israelites, especially by the king, Priests, and the false prophets. Why? Because he spoke what JOVA God gave him to speak.

Now all the words of Jeremiah came to pass, and thus the desolation of the Nation Israel, the Holy City Jerusalem, and the Temple, because they would not repent and amend their ways to the Law of God.

JEREMIAH 29:1
Under Captivity
Verse 1. **NOW these are the words of the letter that Jeremiah the prophet sent from Jerusalem unto the residue of the elders which were carried away captives, and to the priests, and to the prophets, and to all the people whom Nebuchadnezzar had carried away captive from Jerusalem to Babylon.**

EZEKIEL 14:12-23
Repentance
Verse 12. The word of the LORD came again to me, saying,

160

Verse 13. Son of man, when the land sinneth against me by trespassing grievously, then will I stretch out mine hand upon it, and will break the staff of the bread thereof, and will send famine upon it, and will cut off man and beast from it:

Verse 14. **Though these three men, Noah, Daniel, and Job, were in it, they should deliver but their own souls by their righteousness, saith the Lord God.**

Verse 15. If I cause noisome beasts to pass through the land, and they spoil it, so that it be desolate, that no man may pass through because of the beasts:

Verse 16. **Though these three men were in it, as I live, saith the Lord GOD, they shall deliver neither sons nor daughters; they only shall be delivered, but the land shall be desolate.**

Verse 17. Or if I bring a sword upon that land, and say, Sword, go through the land; so that I cut off man and beast from it:

Verse 18. **Though these three men were in it, as I live, saith the Lord GOD, they shall deliver neither sons nor daughters, but they only shall be delivered themselves**.

Verse 19. Or if I send a pestilence into that land, and pour out my fury upon it in blood, to cut off from it man and beast:

Verse 20. **Though Noah, Daniel, and Job, were in it, as I live, saith the Lord GOD, they shall deliver neither son nor daughter; they shall but deliver their own souls by their righteousness**.

Verse 21. For thus saith the Lord GOD; How much more when I send my four sore judgments upon Jerusalem, **the sword**, and the famine, and **the noisome beast**, and **the pestilence**, to cut off from it man and beast?

Verse 22. **Yet, behold, therein shall be left a remnant that shall be brought forth**, both sons and daughters: behold, they shall come forth unto you, and ye shall see their way and their doings: and ye shall be comforted concerning the evil that I have brought upon Jerusalem, even concerning all that I have brought upon it.

Verse 23. And they shall comfort you, when ye see their ways and their doings: **and ye shall know that I have not done without cause all that I have done in it, saith the Lord GOD.**

One could spend so much time looking at all the reasons for the desolation of the first temple. But in a nutshell, the children of Israel would not take heed to correction to repent and amend their ways, and follow God's law. Now it is time to look at the desolation of the second temple, the very temple where the priests despised Christ's Ministry. Jesus established and taught the Law of Love during His time in Israel.

Gospel of the Holy Twelve
Lection LI:12-18.
The Truth Maketh Free
Verse 12. And certain of the Elders and Scribes from the Temple came unto him saying, [Why do thy disciples teach men that it is unlawful to eat the flesh of beasts though they be offered in sacrifice as by Moses ordained.]
Verse 13. **For it is written, God said to Noah, The fear and the dread of you shall be upon every beast of the field, and every bird of the air, and every fish of the sea, into your hand they are delivered.** *(We can find in our Bible today from the K.J.V. the corrupted verse the Elders and Scribes quoted to Jesus. Found in* GENESIS 9:2. *Now back to The Gospel of the Holy Twelve.)*
Verse 14. **And Jesus said unto them, ye hypocrites, well did Esaias speak of you, and your forefathers, sayings This people draweth nigh unto Me, with their mouths, and honour me with their lips, but their heart is far from me, for in vain do they worship Me teaching and believing, and teaching for divine doctrines, the commandments of men in my name but to satisfy their own lusts.** *(Jesus was quoting Isaiah which can be found truthfully written, in The Bible K.J.V. in ISAIAH 29:13. Back to The Gospel of the Holy Twelve.)*

162

Verse 15. As also Jeremiah bear witness when he saith, concerning blood offerings and sacrifices **I the Lord God commanded none of these things in the day that ye came out of Egypt, but only this I commanded you to do, righteousness, walk in the ancient paths, do justice, love mercy, and walk humbly with they God.** *(Jesus had been quoting Jeremiah, the True prophet's words, which were given to him by God's Holy Spirit. These correct scriptures are in JEREMIAH 29:22-23)*

Verse 16. [But ye did not hearken to Me,] **Who in the beginning gave you all manner of seed, and fruit of the trees and seed having been for the food and healing of man and beast.** And they said, Thou speakest against the law. *(Jesus was quoting God's original Word's found in GENESIS 1:29-31)*

Verse 17. **And He said against Moses indeed I do not speak nor against the law, but against them who corrupted his law,** which he permitted for the hardness of your hearts.

Verse 18. But, behold, a greater than Moses is here! And they were wrath and took up stones to cast at him. And Jesus passed through their midst and was hidden from their violence.

Jesus made the point clear, man corrupted Moses commandments to satisfy their own lusts! Christ's disciple, Peter, in the Clementine Homilies, also speaks of the same corruption.

THE CLEMENTINE HOMILIES
Chapter XLVII
Foreknowledge of Moses
Then said Peter: **"The law of God was given by Moses, without writing, to seventy wise men, to be handed down, that the government might be carried on by succession.** *(This can be found in NUMBERS 11:6-35. Seventy wise men chosen to help Moses. And at a place called Kibrothhattaavah, where they buried the people that lusted after flesh.)* But after that Moses was taken up, it was

written by someone, but not by Moses. For in the law itself it is written, 'And Moses died; and they buried him near the house of Phogor, and no one knows his sepulchre till this day.' But how could Moses write that Moses died? And whereas in the time after Moses, about 500 years or thereabouts, it is found lying in the temple which was built, and after about 500 years more it is carried away, and being burnt in the time of Nebuchadnezzar it is destroyed; and thus being written after Moses, and often lost, even this shows the foreknowledge of Moses, because he, foreseeing its disappearance, did not write it; but this who wrote it, being convicted of ignorance through their not foreseeing its disappearance, were not prophets."

One must understand that there are two different doctrines in place in our Christian Bibles today. One version is counterfeit, and the other is genuine, that is, that which is left of the genuine. Peter, Christ's disciple, made this statement about the Old Testament scriptures.

THE CLEMENTINE HOMILIES
Chapter XX
Some parts of the Old Testament written to try us.
"But one might with good reason maintain that it was with reference to those who thought Him to be such that the statement was made, **'No one knoweth the Father but the Son, as no knoweth even the Son, but the Father.'** And reasonably. [For if they had known, they would not have sinned, by trusting to the books written against God, really for the purpose of trying]."

He says, wishing to exhibit the cause of their error more distinctly to them,

"On this account ye do err, not knowing the true things of the Scriptures, on which account ye are ignorant also of the power of God.' Wherefore every man who wishes to be saved must become, as the Teacher said, a judge of the books written to try us. For thus He spake: 'Become experienced bankers.' **Now the need of bankers arises from the circumstance that the spurious, (counterfeit***)* **is mixed up with the genuine."**

Christ Made this statement, knowing His doctrine would be tampered with also.

Gospel of the Holy Twelve
Lection XLIV:5-10
The Confession of the Twelve Christ the True Rock
Verse 5. [Ye are my chosen twelve. In me, the Head and Corner stone, are the twelve foundations of my house builded on the rock, and on you in me shall my Church be built, and in truth and righteosness shall my Church be established.]
Verse 6. And ye shall sit on twelve thrones and send forth light and truth to all the twelve tribes of Israel after the Spirit, and I will be with you, even unto the end of the world.
Verse 7. **But there shall arise after you, men of perverse minds who shall through ignorance or through craft, suppress many things which I have spoken unto you, and lay to me things which I never taught, sowing tares among the good wheat which I have given you to sow in the world.**
Verse 8. [Then shall the truth of God endure the contradiction of sinners, for thus it hath been, and thus it will be]. **But the time cometh when the things which they have hidden shall be revealed and made known, and the truth shall make free those which were bound**.
Verse 9. One is your Master, all ye are brethren, and one is not greater than another in the place which I have given unto you, for ye have one Master, even Christ, who is over you and with you and in you, and there is no inequality among my twelve, or their fellows.
Verse 10. Strive ye not therefore for the first place, for ye are all first, **because ye are the foundation stones and pillars of the Church, built on the truth which is in me**

165

and in you, and the truth and the law shall ye establish for all, as shall be given unto you.

Christ's disciple, Peter, who is a rock from the Rock, also testifies to the corruption that is taking place by lawless men, who proclaim to be teachers of righteousness in his day, after Christ ascended back to the Kingdom of God, after his resurrection.

THE CLEMENTINE HOMILIES
EPISTLE OF PETER TO JAMES
Chapter II
Misrepresentation of Peter's doctrine.

In order, therefore, that the like may also happen to those among us as to these Seventy, give the books of my preachings to our brethren, with the like mystery of initiation, that they may indoctrinate those who wish to take part in teaching; **for if it be not so done, our word of truth will be rent into many opinions. And this I know, not as being a prophet, but as already seeing the beginning of this very evil.** [For some from among the Gentiles have rejected my legal preaching, attaching themselves to certain lawless and trifling preaching of the man who is my enemy.] **And these things some have attempted while I am still alive, to transform my words by certain various interpretations in order to the dissolution of the law; as though I also myself were of such a mind, but did not freely proclaim it, which God forbid!** [For such a thing were to act in opposition to the law of God which was spoken by Moses, and was borne witness to by our Lord in respect of its eternal continuance;] for thus He spoke: **"the heavens and the earth shall pass away, but one jot or one tittle shall in no wise pass from the law."** and this He has said, that all things might come to pass. But these men, professing, I know not how, to know my mind, undertake to explain my words, which they have heard of me, more intelligently than I who spoke them, telling their catechumens that this is my meaning, which indeed I never thought of. **But if,**

while I am still alive, they dare thus to misrepresent me, how much more will those who shall come after me dare to do so!

Again, Peter, Christ's disciple, knew and preached the Lords Law of Love. And he was already seeing the early corruption of his Holy Teachers doctrine, by counterfeit preachers, proclaiming to be teachers of righteousness.

As Christ made the statement: **the heavens and the earth shall pass away, but one jot or one tittle shall in no wise pass from the law.** So where in the New Testament from our Bible today, can we find our Lord's precious Law of Love? You can not, because it has been done away with by the corrupters! Christ stormed the temple shortly before His crucifixion and said:

MATTHEW 21:13. It is written, My house shall be called the house of prayer; but ye have made it a den of thieves.

Now I will quote from the Gospel of the Holy twelve, because I believe it is a much better text in the explanation of the wrongful blood of the innocent animals used in sacrifice, and the evil intent of the people in charge of the Temple. As you will see below, by that which Christ said in His Gospel, Gospel of the Holy Twelve, Lection XXXIII:1-10, By the shedding of blood of others is no remission for sins. His words are at complete odds with what the corrupters wrote in LEVITICUS, Chapters 1 through 7, that declared Moses received from God the laws and rituals for the animal sacrificial offerings. I urge you to read Lection XXXIII:1-10, and know for yourself how it condemn the bloody chapters of Leviticus 1:1-7.

Gospel of the Holy Twelve
Lection LXXI:1-4 & Verse 8
The Cleansing of The Temple
Verse 1. **AND the Jews' Passover was at hand**, and Jesus went up again from Bethany into Jerusalem. And he found

in the temple those that sold oxen and sheep and doves, and the changers of money sitting.

Verse 2. And when he had made a scourge of seven cords, he drove them all out of the temple and loosed the sheep and the oxen, and the doves, and poured out the changers; money, and overthrew the tables;

Verse 3. And said unto them, **Take these things hence; make not my Father's House an House of merchandise. Is it not written, My House is a House of prayer, for all nations? But ye have made it a den of thieves, and filled it with all manner of abominations.**

Verse 4. **And he would not suffer that any man should carry any vessel of blood through the temple, or that any animals should be slain**. And the disciples remembered that it was written, Zeal for thine house hath eaten me up.

Verse 8. **But the scribes and the priests saw and heard, and were astonished and sought how they might destroy him**, for they feared him, seeing that all the people were attentive to his doctrines.

I want to bring in a very important scripture the Holy Spirit has guided me to share. It is about a man named Nathanael who according to our Lord Jesus was already under the symbolic Fig Tree. Nathanael had to have been following Moses uncorrupted law that Moses received on the mount in his day, which would allow Jesus to make such a statement about him.

JOHN 1:43-51

Jesus see's Nathanael under the Fig Tree

Verse 43. The day following Jesus would go forth into Galilee, and findeth Philip, and saith unto him, Follow me.

Verse 44. Now Philip was of Bethsaida, the city of Andrew and Peter.

Verse 45. Philip findeth Nathanael, and saith unto him, We have found him, of whom Moses in the law, and the prophets, did write, Jesus of Nazareth, the son of Joseph.

Verse 46. And Nathanael said unto him, Can there any good thing come out of Nazareth? Philip saith unto him, Come and see.

Verse 47. Jesus saw Nathanael coming to him, and saith of him, **Behold an Israelite indeed, in whom is no guile!**

Verse 48. Nathanael saith unto him, Whence knowest thou me? **Jesus answered and said unto him, Before that Philip called thee, when thou wast under the fig tree, I saw thee.**

Verse 49. Nathanael answered and saith unto him, Rabbi, thou art the Son of God; thou art the King of Israel.

Verse. 50. Jesus answered and said unto him, Because I said unto thee, I saw thee under the fig tree, believest thou? Thou shalt see greater things than these.

Verse 51. And he saith unto him, Verily verily, I say unto you, Hereafter ye shall see heaven open, and the angels of God ascending and descending upon the Son of man.

Jesus said to Nathanael in verse 47. **Behold an Israelite indeed, in whom is no guile.** Remember what Christ said about who was a true Israelite?

Gospel of the Holy Twelve
Lection XLVI:8.
The Giving of the Law
Verse 8. **For who are the Israel of God? Even they of every nation and tribe who work righteousness, love mercy and keep my commandments, [these are the true Israel of God].**

As Jesus spoke to the Elders and Scribes from the Temple, they asked Jesus why His disciples taught men that it is unlawful to eat the flesh, though they be offered in sacrifice as Moses ordained. Jesus quickly spoke out against their corruption of Moses law, which they were practicing in the Second temple. And just like in the first temple, it had become corrupted by counterfeit doctrines - the commandments of men, in God's name, to satisfy their own lusts.

169

Jesus went on to say: Against Moses indeed I do not speak nor against the law, but against them who corrupted his law, which he permitted for the hardness of your hearts. But behold, a greater than Moses is here. I quoted most of these verses of Scripture from The Gospel of the Holy Twelve, Lection LI:12-18. I did such, so one would understand God's Law was never intended to be mixed up with blood sacrifices of any kind. Keep this in mind, because it has monumental importance that is relevant to that which most of the Christian Churches teach today, and that is their version of Christ.

Now Jesus observes the Passover with His disciples.
Gospel of the Holy Twelve
Lection LXXV:4-18
The Last Paschal Supper
Verse 4. **And Jesus said, With desire have I desired to eat this Passover with you before I suffer.** [And to institute the Memorial of my Oblation for the service and salvation of all.] For behold the hour cometh when the Son of man shall be betrayed into the hands of sinners.
Verse 5. And one of the twelve said unto him, Lord, is it I? And he answered, He to whom I give the sop the same is he.
Verse 6. [And Iscariot said unto him, Master, behold the unleaven bread, the mingled wine and the oil and the herbs, **but where is the lamb that Moses commanded?]** (for Judas had bought the lamb, **but Jesus had forbidden that it should be killed**).
Verse 7. And John spake in the Spirit, saying, Behold the Lamb of God, the good Shepherd which giveth his life for the sheep. And Judas was troubled at these words, for he knew that he should betray him. But again Judas said, Master, is it not written in the law that a lamb must be slain for the Passover within the gates?
Verse 8. And Jesus answered, If I am lifted up on the cross then indeed shall the lamb be slain; but woe unto him by

170

whom it is delivered into the hands of the slayers; it were better of him had he not been born.

Verse 9. **Verily I say unto you, for this end have I come into the world, that I may put away all blood offerings and the eating of the flesh of the beasts and the birds that are slain by men.**

Verse 10. **In the beginning, God gave to all, the fruits of the trees, and the seeds, and the herbs, for food; but those who loved themselves more than God, or their fellows, corrupted their ways, and brought diseases into their bodies, and filled the earth with lust and violence.**

Verse 11. **Not by shedding innocent blood, therefore, but by living a righteous life, shall ye find the peace of God.** [Ye call me the Christ of God and ye say well, for I am the Way, the Truth and the Life.

Verse 12. Walk ye in the Way, and ye shall find God. Seek ye the Truth, and the Truth shall make you free. Live in the Life, and ye shall see no death. All things are alive in God, and the Spirit of God filleth all things.

Verse 13. Keep ye the commandments. Love thy God with all thy heart, and love thy neighbour as thyself. On these hang all the law and the prophets. And the sum of the law is this--Do not ye unto others as ye would not that others should do unto you. Do ye unto others, as ye would that others should do unto you.

Verse 14. Blessed are they who keep this law, for God is Manifested in all creatures. All creatures live in God, and God is hid in them.

Verse 15. After these things, Jesus dipped the sop and gave it to Judas Iscariot, saying, What thou doest, do quickly. He then, having received the sop, went out immediately, and it was light.

Verse 16. And when Judas Iscariot had gone out, Jesus said, Now is the Son of man glorified among his twelve, and God is glorified in him. And verily I say unto you, they who receive you receive me, and they who receive me receive the Father-Mother Who sent me, and ye who have been faithful unto the truth shall sit upon twelve thrones, judging the twelve tribes of Israel.

Verse 17. And one said unto him, Lord, wilt thou at this time restore the kingdom unto Israel? **And Jesus said, My kingdom is not of this world, neither are all Israel which are called Israel.**

Verse 18. [They in every nation who defile not themselves with cruelty, who do righteousness, love mercy, and reverence all the works of God, who give succour to all that are weak and oppressed--the same are the Israel of God].

MATTHEW 23:37-38
Prophecy of Destruction
Verse 37. O Jerusalem, Jerusalem, thou that killest the prophets, and stonest them which are sent unto thee, how often would I have gathered thy children together, even as a hen gathered her chickens under her wings, and ye would not!

Verse 38. **Behold, your house is left unto you desolate.**

MATTHEW 24:1-2
Verse 1. **AND Jesus went out, and departed from the temple**: and his disciples came to him for to shew him the buildings of the temple.

Verse 2. **And Jesus said unto them, See ye not all these things? Verily I say unto you, There shall not be left here one stone upon another, that shall not be thrown down..**

In 70 A.D. Jesus' prophecy came to pass; the destruction of the temple and the crushing of Israel as a nation; they were not a nation again, until 1948. *Thus the destruction of the second temple.* Jesus said these words to His disciples shortly before he was put to death, for preaching the Law of Love.

Gospel of the Holy Twelve
Lection LXXVI:5-7
The Washing Of The Feet The Eucharistic Oblation
Verse 5. [A new commandment I give unto you, that ye love one another and all the creatures of God]. **Love is the**

172

fulfilling of the law. [Love is of God, and God is love. Whoso loveth not, knoweth not God].

Verse 6. [**Now ye are clean through the word which I have spoken unto you,** By this shall all men know that ye are my disciples if ye have love one to another and shew mercy and love to all creatures of God, especially to those that are weak and oppressed and suffer wrong]. **For the whole earth is filled with dark places of cruelty, and with pain and sorrow, by the selfishness and ignorance of man.**

Verse 7. [I say unto you, Love your enemies, bless them that curse you, **and give them light for their darkness** and let the spirit of love dwell within your hearts, and abound unto all. And again I say unto you, Love one another, and all the creation of God. And when he had finished, they said, Blessed be God].

This was the true doctrine of the Kingdom, brought through the Genuine Christ, which brought about His death by the evil doers of the temple. The Lord Jesus tried to bring unto them light for their darkness, but they rose up against Him, because of it. They killed Him without a just cause. But by the power of JOVA God, our Lord Jesus rose on the third day, and was seen by many until He ascended back to our Great Creators Kingdom.

Now in our generation because of the abominable acts in God's house of worship today, we will again see the desolation of the places of worship in our day, and it will come about if we don't repent and amend our ways. The churches as a whole, do not worship God in Spirit, and in truth, the way our precious Lord taught His blessed disciples. They have gone away from Christ's original doctrine. They have embraced the traditions and doctrine of men instead. But before the time of punishment and desolation comes, the True Gospel of the Kingdom will be preached again to this generation, just like in the past.

Disciple Peter made this statement.

173

I PETER 4:17. **For the time is come that judgment must begin at the house of God**: and if it first begin at us, what shall the end be of them that obey not the gospel of God?

This has been told to my brother Russell and me, as Gods two witnesses: The time of judgment is soon to come to our generation. But it is a conditional prophecy. If repentance comes from the Churches that are called by our Lord's name, and they embrace the Law of Love, then they will be spared. It is as simple as that. This time of repentance and amendment to God's Law of Love will be brief, similarly to the time of Christ's ministry to Israel. A mighty army of Gods Elect from the True Church, and the Lords two witnesses will make up this mighty army. This is going to cause a mighty reaction amongst the Churches that are called by our Lords name, just like Christ's ministry did in His day. And this will be its likeness!

Gospel of the Holy 12
Lection 17:13-15
Verse 13. What I tell you in darkness, that speak ye in light when the time cometh: and what ye hear in the ear, that preach ye upon the housetops. **Whosoever therefore shall confess the truth before men, them will I confess also before my Parent Who is in heaven. But whosoever shall deny the truth before men, them will I also deny before my Parent Who is in heaven.** Verse 14. Verily I am come to send peace upon earth, but when I speak, behold a sword followeth. **I am come to unite, but, behold, a man shall be at variance with his father, and the daughter with her mother, and the daughter-in-law with her mother-in-law.** And a man's foes shall be they of his own household. For the unjust cannot mate with them that are just. Verse 15. **They who take not their cross and follow after me are not worthy of me. He that findeth his life shall lose it; and he that loseth his life for my sake, shall find it.**

174

Can you imagine when Jesus True Doctrine storms the Churches in our day. This will cause a great shaking among the Churches that are called by our Lords name. Yes, variance is coming. If one embraces the True Doctrine of our Lord Jesus Christ and comes out from the Defiled Church, The Great Whore, then a spiritual seal will be placed upon them. This spiritual seal keeps the true believer from harm, by these stinging creatures.

This scripture came into my mind just as I was writing:

MALACHI 3:16-18
God's Judgement
Verse 16. Then they that feared the LORD spake often one to another: and the LORD hearkened, and heard it, **and a book of remembrance was written before him for them that feared the LORD, and that thought upon his name.**
Verse 17. And they shall be mine, saith the LORD of hosts, in that day when I make up my jewels; **and I will spare them, as a man spareth his own son that serveth him.**
Verse 18. **Then shall ye return, and discern between the righteous and the wicked, between him that serveth God and him that serveth him not.**

I am going to briefly speak about the Defiled Church, The Great Whore, because in previous dreams I already addressed this topic in depth, which Holy Spirit gave me to share. In the Book of Revelation Chapter 17: is where She, The Great Whore is spoken of. I urge you, the reader, to please read Chapter 17, and I pray that your eyes will be opened to the Truth.

First of all, John who was on the Island Patmos, was given this vision. John saw in the vision, starting at Verse 1, seven angels, with seven vials, who talked with him, and said, I will shew you the judgment of the great whore that sitteth upon many waters. Now symbolically, the term many waters, represents many peoples, multitudes, and

175

nations, and tongues, explained in Verse 15, of the same chapter.

Next in Verse 3, John was shown the Great Whore sitting upon a scarlet colored beast, with seven heads and ten horns, full of names of blasphemy. Now the red colored beast is the Dragon, a symbol given to Satan, whom the great Whore rides upon. The seven heads of the Red Dragon, are a symbol for seven mountains on which the woman sitteth. That is found in Verse 9.

The seven mountains, on which the Whore sits, are the seven hills of the Vatican, the Roman headquarters for the Catholic Church, the very Church which Constantine established, mostly from the corrupted doctrine of Apostle Paul. Constantine was emperor of Rome, from A.D. 280-337. And, he converted to a counterfeit Christian belief in the year of A.D. 306. Constantine convened the First Council of Nicaea in the year, 325 A.D., primarily because he feared that disputes within the church would cause disorder within the empire. The bullying actions of those who had the power to do such at the First Council of Nicaea, were responsible for much of the canonization of the Bible we have today. And, I might add: their version of Christ, ties to a blood sacrifice preached by Apostle Paul.

In Verse 6, The Great Whore is drunk with the blood of the True teachers of righteousness. Meaning, she put many to death who teach the Genuine Gospel of Jesus Christ! Next in Verse 8, the statement is made by the angels that spoke to John when they behold the beast, meaning the Red Dragon whom the great whore rides, that they that dwell upon the earth shall wonder whose names were not written in the book of life. That proves without a shadow of a doubt the great whore is a counterfeit church.

Now the ten horns, which are part of the beast system, are described as ten kings. They give their power unto the beast as one mind. And the ten kings, will bring upon the whore

176

great desolation because of her abominations. You can read about the Defiled bride, the Great Whore, and her demise in Verses 12 through 18. In that portion of scripture, which I am about to write, is where Christ's Disciple John, is imprisoned on the Island of Patmos, because of the True testimony of Jesus Christ. And what John was shown, as unto the creature I was shown, they both seem to be very similar in appearance.

The time span concerning the dream I received, must be understood as being shortly before our Lords return for His Holy Bride, His True Church, and those who have kept His commandments and followed the Law of Love. Keep in mind, most of the Churches that are called by our Lord's name today, consume flesh in their homes, and at the Churches banquet tables. They also believe that the precious blood of Christ washes away their sins, if they confess their sins and believe in Him as their Savior. It is extremely important for one to understand that it is only by obeying Christ's Law of Love that salvation can be achieved, for Jesus taught the innocent blood of others does not save one from their sin; only repentance and amendment one's behavior to obeying God's Law of Love, will do such.

This true doctrine of our Lord Jesus Christ, as I said earlier, will cause turmoil and variance amongst the Churches. But keep this in mind, the Lord is going to send His messengers who will proclaim His Laws, which men have hidden by their traditions, and those that continue to transgress, will suffer greatly.

REVELATION 9:1-12
The Fifth Angel
Verse 1. AND the fifth angel sounded, and I saw a star fall from heaven unto the earth: and to him was given the key of the bottomless pit.

Verse 2. And he opened the bottomless pit; as the smoke of a great furnace; and the sun and the air were darkened by reason of the smoke of the pit.

Verse 3. And there came out of the smoke locusts upon the earth: and unto them was given power, as the scorpions of the earth have power.

Verse 4. And it was commanded them that they should not hurt the grass of the earth, neither any green thing, neither any tree; **but only those men which have not the seal of God in their foreheads.**

Verse 5. **And to them it was given that they should not kill them, but that they should be tormented five months**: and their torment was as the torment of a scorpion, when he striketh a man.

Verse 6. And in those days shall men seek death, and shall not find it; and shall desire to die, and death shall flee from them.

Verse 7. And the shapes of the locusts were like unto horses prepared unto battle; **and on their heads were as it were crowns like gold, and their faces were as the faces of men**.

Verse 8. **And they had hair as the hair of women, and their teeth were as the teeth of lions.**

Verse 9. **And they had breastplates, as it were breastplates of iron, and the sound of their wings was as the sound of chariots of many horses running to battle.**

Verse 10. And they had tails like unto scorpions, **and there were stings in their tails: and their power was to hurt men five months**.

Verse 11. **And they had a king over them, which is the angel of the bottomless pit**, whose name in the Hebrew tongue is Abaddon, but in the Greek tongue hath his name Apollyon.

Verse 12. One woe is past; and, behold, there come two woes more hereafter.

I must mention here about the two witnesses, because they have their part in this last day True Church of Jesus Christ. Briefly my brother and I are the two witnesses mentioned

178

in Revelation, Chapter 11, and in Zechariah, Chapter 3 and 4. God has called the two witnesses to prophetically guide Christ's True Church into battle against the great whore, which is the counterfeit Church. They are given great power by God to accomplish their task. And if any man tries to harm them during their ministry, Revelation, Chapter 11, Verse 5, reveals this important fact: And if any man will hurt them, fire proceeded out of their mouth, and devoureth their enemies.

Their ministry, according to Revelations, will be three and a-half years, the same time as Christ's Messianic Ministry unto Israel, during the second temple. Remember Christ's ministry at the end, was mostly directed toward the corruption that had been taught and practiced within the temple, by the Priest's, Elders and Scribes. Revelation, Chapter 11, Verse 7 states: At the end of their ministry the beast that ascendeth out of the bottomless pit shall make war against them, and shall overcome them, and kill them. And the Defiled Church will be greatly excited because of their death.

But According to that which John had been shown, that is revealed in Revelation, Chapter 11, Verse 11, And after three days and an half the Spirit of life from God entered into them, and they stood upon their feet; and great fear fell upon them which saw them. The last three verses I will quote from Revelations.

REVELATIION 11:12-14
Verse 12. And they heard a great voice from heaven saying unto them, come up hither. And they ascended up to heaven in a cloud; and their enemies beheld them.
Verse 13. And the same hour was there a great earthquake, and the tenth part of the city fell, and in the earthquake were slain of men seven thousand: and the remnant were affrighted, and gave glory to the God of heaven.
Verse 14. The second woe is past; and, behold, the third woe cometh quickly.

Yes, the two witnesses will have a large part, in this last day Church of Jesus Christ. The rebellious Watchers or Fallen angels who give their power unto the Red Dragon, have their own evil agenda they want to implement upon our earth, and us, meaning human kind. Their evil wisdom is great, and way ahead of the world's wisdom. Without the seal of God in one's mind, which represents the True Knowledge of Gods Kingdom, it will be a cruel and hurtful place to be in the very near future, and many will be tormented by these evil creatures, and many will die in this great struggle for power. Then there will be a great distinction between those that serve God in Spirit and in Truth, and those that don't!

The Defiled Bride, The Great Whore that rides the Red Dragon is going to suffer greatly if she does not repent and embrace the genuine Christ's Doctrine, which teaches salvation only comes by hearing and obeying The Law of Love that Jesus originally taught. Here is another example, about the mark, God told His angels to put upon the heads of those who sigh and cry for all the abominations that were going on in God's house of worship, back in Ezekiel's day. I urge you to read both Chapters 8 and 9, for due to the length of this message, I will write them in part.

EXEKIEL 8: 4-6 & 9:3-5 & 9-11
Ezekiel's Vision Gods Wrath
Chapter 8:4-6
Verse 4. And, behold, the glory of the God of Israel was there, according to the vision that I saw in the plain.
Verse 5. Then said he unto me, Son of man, lift up thine eyes now the way toward the north. So I lifted up mine eyes the way toward the north, and behold northward at the gate of the altar this image of jealousy in the entry.
Verse 6. **He said furthermore unto me, Son of man, seest thou what they do? Even the great abominations that the house of Israel committeth here, that I should go far**

off from my sanctuary? But turn thee yet again, and thou shalt see greater abominations.

Chapter 9:3-5
Verse 3. From: And the glory of the God of Israel was gone up from the cherub, whereupon he was, to the threshold of the house. And he called to the man clothed with linen, which had the writer's inkhorn by his side;
Verse 4. And the LORD said unto him, Go through the midst of the city, through the midst of Jerusalem, and set a mark upon the foreheads of the men that sigh and that cry for all the abominations that be done in the midst thereof.
Verse 5. And to the others he said in mine hearing, Go ye after him through the city, and smite: let not your eye spare, neither have pity:

Chapter 9:9-11
Verse 9. Then said he unto me, The iniquity of the house of Israel and Judah is exceeding great, and the land is full of blood, and the city full of perverseness: for they say, The LORD hath forsaken the earth, and the LORD seeth not.
Verse 10. And as for me also, mine eye shall not spare, neither will I have pity, but I will recompense their way upon their head.
Verse 11. And, behold, the man, *(angel)* clothed with linen, which had the inkhorn by his side, reported the matter, saying, I have done as thou hast commanded me.

ECCLESIASTES 1:9-10
Verse 9. The thing that hath been, it is that which shall be; and that which is done is that which shall be done: and there is no new thing under the sun.
Verse 10. Is there any thing whereof it may be said, See, this is new? It hath been already of old time, which was before us.

MALACHI 3:6
Prophecy of the Forerunner

181

Verse 6. **For I am the LORD, I change not;** therefore ye sons of Jacob are not consumed. (*Jacob's sons, stands for Gods remnant*).

AMOS 3:7
Warnings
Verse 7. **Surely the Lord GOD will do nothing, but he revealeth his secret unto his servants the prophets.**

Gospel of the Holy Twelve
Lection LXVI:1 AGAIN Jesus taught them saying, God hath raised up witnesses to the truth in every nation and every age, **that all might know the will of the Eternal and do it, and after that, enter into the kingdom, to be rulers and workers with the Eternal.**

There will be no excuses, because in our generation God is going to bring forth His glorious House of Worship again. The True Church of Jesus Christ will shine its light of Truth to all the nations, before Christ's soon return for His Holy Bride. The time will be short, but very powerful indeed. Its likeness will be similar to the coming together of the Dry Bones spoken of in EZEKIEL Chapter 37: its early beginnings are happening now!

Reverend Roderick C. Davis, as Head Pontiff, who God has anointed to help bring together Christ's true Church in this last day generation, has been very busy indeed. He has finished a book which he dedicated to God, 'The Miracle of Three Physical Signs from God.' It is a great teaching tool that will help the seekers of truth understand the corruption that has taken place in the Bible we have today. It will prove to the student of God's Word, man corrupted the scriptures, to satisfy his own lusts. And in the works, as Reverend Roderick C. Davis is instructed by the Holy Spirit, is to get his book into free media recognitions in Newspapers, radio and TV, and hopefully, also be a guest on radio and TV talk shows.

Also, God's book, 'The Miracle of Three Physical Signs from God,' was written in a format that would encourage its use in the development of home ministries, both in the United States and around the World. And in the very near future, it will bring together a body of True Spirit Filled believers, in Jesus' World Church, called Unified Church of Christ & Truth. Children of God, the Bride of Christ is making herself ready for her Lovers return!

Gospel of the Holy Twelve
Lection LXX:12-14
Jesus rebukes Peter For His Haste
Verse 12. And one shall sit on my throne, who shall be a Man of Truth and Goodness and Power, and he shall be filled with love and wisdom beyond all others, and shall rule my Church by a fourfold twelve and by two and seventy as of old, and that only which is true shall he teach.
Verse 13. And my Church shall be filled with Light, and give Light unto all nations of the earth, and there shall be one Pontiff sitting on his throne as a King and a Priest.
Verse 14. And my Spirit shall be upon him and his throne shall endure and not be shaken, for it shall be founded on love and truth and equity, and light shall come to it, and go forth from it, to all the nations of the earth, and the Truth shall make them free.

Like in the dream, the end of this age is nearing its climax, but for the followers of God's Law of Love, the best is yet to come. The restoring of the world through Christ will usher in the Time of Rest, The One Thousand Year Reign, also known as The Millennium. Looking forward to this day was the reason for keeping the Sabbath Day Holy. Only those who obeyed God's Law and worshiped the Eternal in Spirit and in Truth, will be allowed in, to rule and reign with Christ our Lord, who is King of kings and Lord of Lords.

Christ our Lord, made this statement as He quoted the words of the prophet Isaiah, found in the ISAIAH Chapter

11, and also in the Gospel of the Holy Twelve, called the Restoration of the World. I will quote from the Gospel of the Holy Twelve.

Gospel of the Holy Twelve
Lection VI:18-20
Verse 18. For the Spirit of Divine Humanity filling him, filled all things around him, and made all things subject unto him, **and thus shall yet be fulfilled the words of the prophets**, the Lion shall lie down with the calf, and the leopard with the kid, and the wolf with the lamb, and the bear with the ass, and the hawk with the dove. And a child shall lead them.
Verse 19. And none shall hurt or destroy in my holy mountain, for the earth shall be full of the knowledge of the Holy One even as the waters cover the bed of the sea. And in that day I will make again a covenant with the beasts of the earth and the fowls of the air, and the fishes of the sea and with all created things. And will break the bow and the sword and all the instruments of warfare will I banish from the earth, and will make them to lie down in safety, and to live without fear.
Verse 20. And I will betroth thee unto me for ever in righteousness and in peace and in loving kindness, and thou shalt know thy God, and the earth shalt bring forth the corn the wine and the oil, and I will say unto them which were not my people, Thou art my people; and they shall say unto me, Thou art our God.

Only the ones who obeyed from the heart, Jesus' true Doctrine, will enter in, to be rulers and reign with Him in the restored earth. The Lord Jesus taught us how to pray, and it is called the Lord 's Prayer, found in MATTHEW 6:9-13: Thy Kingdom come. Thy will be done in earth, as it is in heaven.

However, the Defiled Church does not understand the True Kingdom of God that is coming to our earth through the Genuine Christ. Unfortunately the Defiled Church has

184

believed another Christ's doctrine that allows them to transgress the Holy Law of Love. Their Christ is just another form of a blood covenant. This corrupted scripture ties in the old blood covenant with the new one, through a counterfeit Christ. I urge you to read the whole Hebrews Chapter 9, part of which is below:

HEBREWS 9:19-28
Remission of Sins
Verse 19. For when Moses had spoken every precept to all the people according to the law, he took the blood of calves and of goats, with water, and scarlet wool, and hyssop, and sprinkled both the book, and all the people,

Verse 20, Saying, This is the blood of the testament which God hath enjoined unto you.

Verse 21. Moreover he sprinkled with blood both the tabernacle, and all the vessels of the ministry.

Verse 22.And almost all things are by the law purged with blood; **and without shedding of blood is no remission.**

Verse 23. It was therefore necessary that the patterns of things in the heavens should be purified with these; but the heavenly things themselves with better sacrifices than these.

Verse 24. For Christ is not entered into the holy places made with hands, which are the figures of the true; but into heaven itself, now to appear in the presence of God for us:

Verse 25. Nor yet that he should offer himself often, as the high priest entereth into the holy place every year with blood of others;

Verse 26. For then must he often have suffered since the foundation of the world: but now once in the end of the world hath **he appeared to put away sin by the sacrifice of himself**.

Verse 27. And as it is appointed unto men once to die, but after this the judgment:

Verse 28. So Christ was once offered to bear the sins of many; and unto them that look for him shall he appear the second time without sin unto salvation.

Gospel of the Holy Twelve
Lection LXVI:13.
Jesus teaches In The Palm Circle The Divine Life And Substance
Verse 13. Whoso therefore forsaketh Christ the Saviour, the Holy law, and the body of the Elect, let them die the death. Yea, let them be lost in the outer darkness, for so they willed and none can hinder.

In closing I ask you this: whose report will you believe: That of the false Apostle Paul; or that of Jesus' appointed Apostle, John?

Chapter 19

Barren

I, Paul Maddock, received this dream from the Holy Spirit during the early morning hours of the Sabbath, November 7, 2015. The dream began as the Defiled bride is having great discomfort in her abdominal area. The pain is so intense that she decided to see her Physician. He told her that the pain she is experiencing is due to a severe disease in her reproductive organs. The Great Physician explained to her that she will never again be able to bring forth children.

After hearing that devastating news, she began to cry with sadness. But soon her sadness turned into anger, which she soon directed toward me. Then, while holding onto a golden cylinder that was full of clear water, the Defiled Bride began to walk toward me. The golden cylinder, about 14 inches long, had a handle attached to it, and about as big around as a common dinner plate.

As the Defiled Bride made her way to me, I noticed she had a white stone in her right hand, which was about the size of a major league baseball, except it was more oval in shape. Her face radiated pure anger as she set the golden cylinder on the ground in front of me, and she immediately tossed the white stone into the clear water, causing a big splash, after which she then said, "I mostly blame you for my condition," and with that statement the dream ended.

Holy Spirit Gave Meaning to the Dream

The Defiled Bride and the Great Whore are one in the same. She is spoken of in this symbolic manner because she is the defiled Church that has left her first love (Jesus and His doctrine), and has embraced another lovers doctrine. That lover is spiritually identified as the scarlet colored beast which she rides, and he is the authority and power of the Anti-Christ that resides in the Roman Catholic Church. And, it is Roman Catholic Church counterfeit doctrine that she now loves and teaches.

Note: The messages verses/lessons contained in the Old and New Testaments of the Catholic Bible, Douay Version, and King James Bible, KJV, which were printed during the same era, are virtually the same. The King James Bible, KJV, will be quoted throughout the rest of this writing.

REVELATION 17:5 & 9
Verse 5. And upon her forehead was a name written, MYSTERY, BABYLON THE GREAT, **THE MOTHER OF HARLOTS** AND ABOMINATIONS OF THE EARTH.
Verse 9. And here is the mind which hath wisdom. The seven heads **are seven mountains**, on which the woman sitteth.

That Verse points to the exact mountain range which surrounds the Vatican. And it is the world capital of the Roman Catholic Church - The Great Whore! Out from her came many other Protestant Churches - Her Children. Now they have one common belief that their Savior Jesus Christ had been a blood sacrifice for their sins, which is called a Vicarious Atonement. In other words, they teach the innocent Christ suffered and died for their sins, which made Him into a blood sacrifice, for the sins of many.

That is a big lie! Why? Jesus did not preach that He'd be a sacrifice to redeem mankind from their sin, only the counterfeit doctrine of the Roman Catholic Church, and Her Children, the Protestant Churches, teaches such. Salvation can be achieved, only by obeying our Lord's Twelve Laws of Love, which the Roman Catholic Church has done away with. It is only by knowing and amending one's ways to those Laws, coupled with repentance, does one achieve salvation.

Our Lord's precious Laws were recorded by Apostle John, in a writing now known as The Gospel of the Holy Twelve, and they are in Lection XLVI:10-21

10. "Ye shall not take away the life of any creature for your pleasure, nor for your profit, nor yet torment it.

11. "Ye shall not steal the goods of any, nor gather lands and riches to yourselves, beyond your need or use.

12. "Ye shall not eat the flesh, nor drink the blood of any slaughtered creature, nor yet anything which bringeth disorder to your health or senses.

13. "Ye shall not make impure marriages, where love and health are not, nor yet corrupt yourselves, or any creature made pure by the Holy.

14. "Ye shall not bear false witness against any, nor willfully deceive any by a lie to hurt them.

15. "Ye shall not do unto others, as ye would not that others should do unto you.

16. "Ye shall worship One Eternal, the Father-Mother in Heaven, of Whom are all things, and reverence the holy Name.

17. "Ye shall revere your fathers and your mothers on earth, whose care is for you, and all the 'Teachers of Righteousness.'

18. "Ye shall cherish and protect the weak, and those who are oppressed, and all creatures that suffer wrong.

19. "Ye shall work with your hands the things that are good and seemly; so shalt ye eat the fruits of the earth, and live long in the land.

20. "Ye shall purify yourselves daily, and rest the Seventh Day from labour, keeping holy the Sabbaths, and the Festival of your God.

21. "Ye shall do unto others as ye would that others should do unto you."

Further to the Laws Jesus gave, it is stated in MATTHEW 5:18, which is part of Jesus' *Sermon on the Mount*: For verily I say unto you, Till heaven and earth pass, one jot or one tittle shall in no wise pass from the law, till all be fulfilled.

Below is an example of the Great Whore's doctrine.

COLOSSIANS 2:14, *Established in the faith*: Blotting out the handwriting of ordinances that was against us, which was contrary to us, and took it out of the way, nailing it to his cross.

Next, I quote the Great Physician spoken of in the dream, who is none other than our Messiah, Jesus Christ.
MATTHEW Verse 12-13.
Verse 12. But when Jesus heard that, he said unto them, **They that be whole need not a physician, but they that are sick.**
Verse 13. **But go ye and learn what that meaneth, I will have mercy, and not sacrifice:** for I am not come to call the righteous, **but sinners to repentance.**

Jesus explained in Verse 13, who the sick really are. They were the ones who transgress His Law. Again, if you believe the defiled doctrine of the Great Whore who has done away with our Messiahs Law, and has replaced it with their version of Christ as a blood sacrifice for the forgiveness of sin, then you are truly spiritually sick.

Gospel of the Holy Twelve

190

Lection XXXIII:1-3
By The Shedding Of Blood Of Others Is No Remission Of Sins

Verse 1. JESUS was teaching his disciples in the outer court of the Temple and one of them said into him: Master, it is said by the priests that without shedding of blood there is no remission. Can then the blood offering of the law take away sin?

Verse 2. And Jesus answered: **No blood offering, of beast or bird, or man, can take away sin, for how can the conscience be purged from sin by the shedding of innocent blood? Nay, it will increase the condemnation.**

Verse 3. The priests indeed receive such offering as a reconciliation of the worshippers for the trespasses against the law of Moses, **but for sins against the Law of God there can be no remission, save by repentance and amendment.**

Again, only by knowing the Law of Love, and by repenting, and by amending ones ways to it, can one achieve salvation. God's two witnesses are prophesied to come as the forerunners of Christ, just before our Lords second return for His Holy Church. This last day Church is faithful to His teaching, and have kept themselves pure like a Virgin Bride. God sends His Two last day prophets to reestablish the Messiahs Law, which the Great Whore has deceitfully done away with. And their message will be clear: Repent and amend your ways or else Gods judgment is soon to come. And, He gives them great power to do so.

Also a great army of true believers will be gathered around them, as the Two Witnesses lead them into battle against the Great Whore, and her counterfeit doctrine. The Two Witnesses will be part of the Last Day Church that is without spot, wrinkle or blemish. Now, out from the Defiled Church of Rome will come a great speaker. He comes upon the scene as nation shall rise against nation, and Kingdom against Kingdom: (Light against Darkness), and there shall be famines, and pestilences, and earthquakes, in divers places. He will be the last Ant-Christ, of the soon to end Church age.

Refer to DANIEL 11:24-45 & DANIEL 12. The Two Witnesses and the true Church of Christ will trouble the Great Whore and Her Churches greatly, because they will expose her evil ways to the world, and call her to repentance. No sign shall be given unto this last day evil generation, except for the sign of the Jonah. Scripture reference from the Bible in the book of MATTHEW 16:4, and also in the Gospel of the Holy Twelve, Lection XLV:1-3.

As Jonas was swallowed by the great fish, which is a symbol for Christ, he was taken to the shores of the great city of Nineveh to deliver a message of repentance to them, or face Gods judgment, and thankfully they did repent. Scripture reference from the Bible, the book of JONAH. The Two Witnesses are the lesser fish sent to this evil generation by the greater fish, Jesus, to call all to repentance, including the unjust. And they know that God's judgment is soon to come upon the ungodly.

I was given a dream by Holy Spirit which explained this, which is titled: My Two Witnesses, which can be read within RodCDavis.com, thru the "God & the Holy Spirit, Prophetic Visions & Dreams, button, found as you scroll down the home page. The Two Witnesses will expose the workings of the Evil One's Church. Also I would like to point the reader to a dream my brother Russell received by the Holy Spirit Titled: Speaking for the Animals, The Dream of the Goose. It represents our mission as Gods Two Messengers of Christ Jesus' Truth concerning the innocent creatures of God. It can also be read on RodCDavis.com, along with many more of our dreams and visions.

And, now I will provide the explanation of the final symbols that were given in the dream, plus the scriptures that correspond to Jesus' last day Church. Remember, the

192

Holy Bride Church listens to the Two Witnesses, and is drawn to them as the forerunners of our soon coming Lord and King! The meaning of Gold Cylinder:

REVELATION 3:18-19
To the Churches
Verse 18. I counsel thee to buy of me **gold tried in fire**,(all dross removed), that thou mayest be rich; and white raiment, that thou mayest be clothed, and that the shame of thy nakedness do not appear; **and anoint thine eyes with eye-salve, that thou mayest see**. (Again the Great Physician)
Verse 19. As many as I love, I rebuke and chasten: be zealous therefore, and repent.

The meaning of the small body of clear water inside the Golden Cylinder

REVELATION 4:6, *Vision of God's Throne*: And before the throne there was a sea of glass like unto crystal:

The sea of glass like unto crystal is the accumulating of the saints throughout all the different ages who upheld and loved the Word of Gods Law. And our Messiah's last day Holy Bride Church, although small in number, will be added into that crystal sea as well. The Defiled Churches' population will be unfortunately much greater than that of our Lords Last Day Church. Again, a distinct body of water is symbolically shown to show its size.

REVELATION 17:15, *Woman in Purple*: And he saith unto me, **The waters which thou sawest, where the whore sitteth, are peoples, and multitudes, and nations, and tongues.**

The meaning of the White Stone
REVELATION 2:17, *To the Churches*: He that hath an ear, let him hear what the Spirit saith unto the Churches; To him that overcometh will I give to eat of the hidden manna,

193

and will give him a white stone, and in the stone a new name written, which no man knoweth saving he that receiveth it.

Those symbols represent the ones that have become pure by obeying our Lords genuine doctrine, and our Messiah's precious doctrine was firmly established upon the Law of Love. The Two Witnesses of Yahshua will lead the Holy Bride Church into battle against the Great Whore's deceitful ways, and will again establish to this last day generation, in a mighty way, our Lord's Law, which is symbolically portrayed as the Plumb line. Refer to ZECHARIAH 4:10 in the Bible.

At the end of the dream the Defiled Bride places the golden cylinder, which held the clear water, down in front of me, and then with disgust, she dropped in the white stone that caused the splash. That represents her strong rejection and hatred toward the Two Witnesses' ministry, and what they stand for. They have caused her much torment by exposing her ways. Eventually after three and a half years of their ministry, they will be killed by the beast that ascendeth out of the bottomless pit, which the Great Whore rides. The length of the Two Witnesses' ministry is identical to that of their precious Lords ministry to Israel. And, their death and resurrection after three and a half days, is again identical to that of Jesus, and will prove without a shadow of doubt, their authenticity. Refer to REVELATION 11.

Shortly thereafter, the Lord gathers His Holy Church, His Bride, and the great tribulation begins. Refer to REVELATION 19:7-9. During this time there will be those who now realize the Two Witnesses' ministry is the genuine teachings of Christ. But unfortunately, they will have to endure the great storm of the tribulation. They will still have a chance to earn salvation by obeying the Messiah's Law, but because they were stiff necked and hard hearted, it will be terrible for most of them, to say the least. Refer to REVELATION 7:14.

194

The whole world is going to hear the true Gospel of Jesus Christ; there will be no excuses. Refer to the Gospel of the Holy Twelve, Jesus Foretelleth The End, Lection LXI:5, and please read the whole chapter. The punishment for the cruel and loveless during this time will be horrendous, and the Great Whore and her children will not escape the wrath of God. Eventually the Great Whore will be destroyed by the Beast and his evil empire, and she will never give birth to children again! Yes, her lover will turn upon her in his wrath. Refer to REVELATION Chapters 17 & 18.

Right now it would take up too much space to write in the many scriptures concerning this message. But if you go to RodCDavis.com, you will find our Holy Spirit given dreams and visions. And they will have the scriptures there for you to follow. Our Messiah's Bride is making herself ready for Her Lord's soon return, and the wedding. The Lord's last day Church already has its anointed man of God as Head Pontiff. And that man is Reverend Roderick C. Davis.

What the Lord and Holy Spirit have already done through this man, is incredible to say the least! Things are beginning to come together quickly. The true body of Christ is being prepared for the great battle that lies ahead. Not one word of God's Two prophets will fall to the ground. For the words they speak are not their own, but they are the words of one much greater, THE WORD OF GOD, and of the Messiah, Jesus Christ.

In closing, Jesus heart felt words to the defiled Churches.

REVELATION 18:4 And I heard another voice from heaven, saying, Come out of her, my people, that ye be not partakers of her sins, and that ye receive not of her plagues.

REVELATION 17:8 The beast that thou sawest was, and is not; and shall ascend out of the bottomless pit, and go into perdition: **and they that dwell on the earth shall wonder, whose names were not written in the book of life from the foundation of the world,** when they behold the beast that was, and is not, and yet is. Amen and Amen. God's Two Witnesses, Russell and Paul Maddock.

Chapter 20

Resources for Further Study, and Other Information

As mentioned in the 'Preface,' the referenced resources identified in the Homilies of Reverend Roderick C. Davis, and also identified in the explanations of the Visions and Dreams given by Holy Spirit, to Russell and Paul Maddock, are available in the Bibliography section of 'The Miracle of Three Physical Signs from God.'

Take look inside of 'The Miracle of Three Physical Signs from God' thru this link:
http://www.rodcdavis.com/Sample-Chapters---The-Miracle-of-Three-Physical-Signs.html

Directions to purchase 'The Miracle of Three Physical Signs from God' are available thru this link:
http://www.rodcdavis.com/Purchase-Printed-Book.html

Learn about Reverend Roderick C. Davis:
http://www.rodcdavis.com/About-Rod-C-Davis.html

Other books by the author:

River of Fear, Encounters: A paranormal action thriller

Communicating with the Other Side: Educational

YouTube Channel:

https://www.youtube.com/user/nvwriter

YouTube Channel contains 30 Video Documentaries by Rev. Roderick C. Davis, which are devoted to revealing lies within the Catholic and King James Bibles.

* 9 7 8 0 9 9 6 3 4 3 4 6 6 *